The PocketScroll® Series

SHAAR PRESS

published by

RABBI ZELIG PLISKIN

GRATITUDE: FORMULAS, STORIES, AND INSIGHTS

Table of Contents

Introduction

What is important to you in your life?

We all want to live happy lives. To live an authentically happy life, we need to be grateful for all the good we experience in life.

As a reader of the material in this book commented, "I had thought of all types of reasons why I wasn't as happy as I wished to be. Now I realize that I was missing gratitude. This is the ingredient that makes all the difference."

We all want to live meaningful lives. To live a truly meaningful life, we need to connect with our Creator. Expressing our gratitude to our Father, our King, Creator and Sustainer of the universe, for all the good He bestows upon us connects us with love and joy.

We all want to live in harmony with the people with whom we interact. When we experience gratitude for all the good that others do for us, we will greatly upgrade the way we interact with those people. This gratitude will prevent us from saying and doing things that could cause distress, and will motivate us to say and do things that will create harmony. Those who experience our gratitude will automatically interact with us in more positive ways.

Gratitude is the fundamental attribute that is a foundation of happiness throughout our lives. Ingratitude causes us to overlook all the good in our lives. Ingratitude is the source of much of the distress in our lives.

Without gratitude, one can have much but live a miserable life. Without gratitude, one won't honor one's parents properly. In a marriage without gratitude, a couple can easily get into many needless quarrels and arguments. Without gratitude, one can pursue wealth or success but won't find fulfillment and satisfaction in anything, regardless of how wealthy or successful one becomes.

Two people can have lives that seem very similar from the outside. They both can have what seems to be a good life. They have nice homes, plenty of food, a fine family, good jobs. Yet the quality of their lives can be polar opposites. One lacks gratitude. He is always dissatisfied and unhappy. He always focuses on what he considers to be missing. He always has complaints. He creates negativity wherever he goes. The other has mastered gratitude. He lives a more spiritual life. He is always grateful and joyful. He always has a good word to say about others. It is a pleasure to be in his company. He is constantly in a state of well-being. He consistently makes others feel good.

If you had to choose between a life with or without gratitude, isn't it obvious what your choice should be? Your rational mind tells you, "Master gratitude!" Will you? Only you can answer this.

After reading this book, your mind will become more aware of how you can be more grateful for more things. You will notice positive things that you hadn't noticed before. You will be more aware of the good that others do for you and have already done for you. You will find your level of happiness increasing. Your love for the Creator will increase. You will always have something to praise Him for.

The thoughts you think create your feelings and emotions. The thoughts you think are the key factor in what you say and do. The entire quality of your life is totally dependent on the thoughts you choose to think. Choose thoughts of gratitude. You will be tremendously grateful that you did.

Gratitude is a source of much light and happiness. Let gratitude transform and elevate your life.

NOTE: The stories presented in this book are about many different people and happened over the course of many years. Care has been taken not to include any information that could identify the subjects.

⋙⋘

I am grateful to the Almighty, our Father, our King, Creator and Sustainer of the universe, for His constant kindness from my first breath until the present.

I am grateful to the entire ArtScroll staff for all they have done to publish this book and my previous ArtScroll books. I am especially grateful to Reb Shmuel Blitz.

I am grateful to my late father, a disciple of the Chofetz Chaim in his yeshiva in Radin. My father's love for Torah, his exemplary character traits, and his wisdom radiated great light.

I am grateful to my mother for her constant love.

I am grateful to my in-laws, Rabbi and Mrs. Simcha Weissman, for all that they have done for our family.

I am grateful to all of my teachers in Talmudical Academy, Telshe Yeshiva, Yeshivas Brisk, and to the many other great teachers whose lectures I merited attending and hearing, especially the late Torah scholars Rabbi Chaim Shmuelevitz, who was the Rosh Hayeshiva of Mir; Rabbi Avigdor Miller; and Rabbi Chaim Zaichyk.

I am grateful to Rabbi Noah Weinberg, the Rosh Hayeshiva of Yeshiva Aish HaTorah, from whom I have gained so much.

I am grateful to my dear friend Rabbi Kalman Packouz for his friendship and encouragement.

I am grateful to my dear brother-in-law, Rabbi Hershel Weizberg, for his ongoing kindness and compassion that is greatly appreciated.

My prayer is: May Hashem continue to bless myself, my wife, and our entire family with the unlimited kindness He has bestowed upon us until now.

1.

Wake Up: You Live in an Amazing, Fantastic World

*W*hat if after you woke up one morning, you were told in the most enthusiastic voice you have ever heard, "Wake up! Wake up! It's wonderful! It's great!"

"What is?" you would ask.

And the voice would tell you, "You live in an amazing, fantastic world."

Would you feel that you were just dreaming? Or would you realize that it's your Creator Who is telling you this each and every day?

The ultimate genius of a Creator created you, and you are in His amazing world. You are a creation of the Creator and you have been blessed by Him.

From the moment you open your eyes until the moment you go to sleep at night you live in a world that has been created for your benefit.

Each and every moment of your life you will have things for which to be grateful. Will you be? That is up to you.

If you think thoughts of gratitude, you will be grateful.

That is your purpose in this world: Recognize your loving Creator and appreciate all that He has done for you. "His kindness is forever" (*Psalms* 136:1). Recognize it. Be grateful for it.

Everyone has much to be grateful for. Gratitude creates happiness and joy. Gratitude helps you be calm and serene. Gratitude helps you connect with and love the Creator. Gratitude elevates your entire life.

"I used to live in a dark world. I didn't realize how needlessly dark it was until I transformed what I saw and realized that I had been living in a world of light the entire time." This was told to me by an elderly gentleman many years ago. He radiated joy. He spoke with a deep sense of compassion and caring for others.

I was fascinated. "Please tell me about your life and how you became the way you are."

"I was a negative person. I easily focused on what was wrong with things. I saw what was wrong with what people did for me, and complained about what they didn't do. There were always things that were missing from what I wanted. I blamed other people for irritating me. Nothing was ever perfect enough. The sentences that would travel through my mind were consistently negative and full of complaints. I felt emotionally distressed most of the time. I felt that I was this way because of my personality, because of the way I was raised, because things are never perfect. But the main place where I didn't look for my sense of happiness and well-being was in my mind.

"Then, one day, my entire world seemed to crumble. I was in a serious car accident. I was told I might not live. That was the most painful thing I had ever heard in my life. It hurt me more than the physical pain. I thought about my entire life. The thought that was the strongest was that I had wasted much of the blessing in my life with my own sense of ingratitude. I was ungrateful to the Creator, ungrateful to the people who did the most for me, and ungrateful to everyone who had done things for me my entire life. I made a commitment that if I would live, I would become a master of gratitude. I would appreciate all that the Almighty keeps giving me. I would appreciate His world. I would appreciate the opportunities He sends my way. I would appreciate everything and anything that anyone has done for me already and would do for me in the future.

"When I came to this realization, I felt lighter. I felt better than I had felt in a long time, even though I was in pain and I didn't know what would happen. I told myself that I wasn't going to make the mistake I had been making my entire life. I wasn't going to say that I will be grateful only if I get better and all is perfect. I wholeheartedly resolved that I would become a totally grateful person from that moment on.

"The recovery period was long. But I felt grateful for every drop of improvement. I needed the kindnesses of others. I was grateful for all that everyone did for me. My entire life was filled with gratitude.

"People told me that they enjoyed being around me. My joyful attitude made them feel good. They were happy to do things for me; they gained by being in my presence, since emotions are contagious. I am grateful to the Almighty for His wake-up call. I am grateful for the flow of spiritual and emotional abundance in my life."

2.

Think, Speak, and Act Like a Grateful Person Does

ere is a one-sentence formula for becoming a grateful person: Think, speak, and act like a grateful person does.

Doesn't this seem obvious? Yes and no. When you think about this rule, yes — it does seem obvious. There is no mystery about how to become a person with the attribute of gratitude. Think gratefully. Speak gratefully. Act gratefully. When you consistently do these three things, you are consistently grateful. And even before this pattern has become consistent for you, every little bit of thinking, speaking, and acting this way makes you more grateful than if you wouldn't have thought, spoken, or acted this way.

The reason why this isn't so obvious is that many people think of gratitude in ways that make it much more complex and difficult than it actually is.

Am I claiming that developing this pattern is easy? No. I'm not claiming that this is easy. And I'm not claiming that this is difficult. If you view it as easy, it will probably be easier for you than it would have been had you viewed it as difficult. If you view it as difficult, it is almost inevitable that it will be more difficult than if you wouldn't have viewed it this way.

There are challenging situations where lack of gratitude is easy and having gratitude is difficult. The more you integrate and internalize the thoughts and attitudes of gratitude, the easier it will be for you to transcend those challenges.

Following this formula for gratitude will help you master all the positive traits and qualities that you wish to master. When you think, speak, and act like a joyful person, you will become a joyful person. When you think, speak, and act like a kind person, you will be kind. When you think, speak, and act like a courageous person, you will be courageous. When you think, speak, and act like a patient person, you will be patient. When you think, speak, and act like a calm and serene person, you will be calm and serene. When you think, speak, and act like an enthusiastic person, you will be enthusiastic. The rest is commentary.

"I was disappointed with myself and felt awful. I should have been much more grateful than I was. The Almighty has given me a multitude of gifts throughout my life. I was better off than billions of people around the world. But was I full of gratitude? Not really. From time to time, I would say, 'I am grateful to the Creator for all His kindnesses,' but I was far from the ideal truly grateful person.

I would frequently complain, 'I'm not as grateful as I should be.' I felt a little better because if I wasn't as grateful as I should be, at least I felt guilty about it. But this pattern of thinking and speaking didn't transform me into a grateful person.

"I mentioned this to the author of this book when he told me that he was writing a book on gratitude. I said, 'I feel so guilty that I'm not as grateful as I should be. Maybe your book will make me more grateful.'

"He said to me, 'My book can't make you grateful. Only you can do that. My book can just give you ideas to think about. Since it will be a while until the book is published, let me give you a concise formula. Apply this and you will be grateful. "Think, speak, and act like a grateful person, and you will become grateful." Apply this, and whether or not you end up reading the book, you will be grateful. Reading the book will help fill your mind with thoughts of gratitude, with ideas about speaking gratefully, and reminders to act gratefully. But it's up to your own thinking, speaking, and acting. Try this for a week and see if you find yourself being a more grateful person.'

"I saw that to the degree that I followed this formula, it worked. It was clear to me that I needed to focus on the right direction: the direction of thinking, speaking, and acting with gratitude."

3.

You Will Notice What You Are Looking For

*M*ake it your goal to build up the attribute of gratitude and you will find that you will notice more things for which to be grateful.

As we have pointed out many times in previous books: Whatever it is that you resolve to notice, that is what you will notice. It then becomes important to you, and what is important to you, you will notice.

An often-cited example is that if someone's name gets mentioned in a large, crowded, noisy room, the person will hear it louder and clearer than anything else that is said. This is so even if he was far away from the conversation and wasn't consciously trying to listen to what was being said. One's name represents oneself, and therefore one's mind notices it.

Similarly, someone who loves birds will notice them when most people wouldn't have seen them. Someone who loves flowers notices them even though others would just pass them by without registering them. Someone who is looking for things to complain about will notice what he is looking for. And someone who hates litter will see the litter rather than seeing the birds and the flowers.

Make it important to be grateful. Then you will notice more and more things that others do for you. You might wonder why it is that more people are doing more things for you. In reality, it could be the same amount as before, but now you notice it.

Now you will notice smiles that make you feel better. And you will be grateful for those smiles. You will notice when people offer you something to eat or drink. You will notice information that people share with you because they feel you will benefit from it. You will notice minor acts of kindness that would not otherwise have registered on your consciousness.

Moreover, you will notice more expressions of gratitude said or done by others. You will hear people mentioning that they received this or that gift because of someone's gratitude. These will serve as reminders for you to do similar things because of gratitude.

When you make it your business to become a more grateful person, your entire world will be filled with more gratitude.

I met a fellow whom I hadn't seen in over five years. The last time I had seen him he was pessimistic, negative, miserable, and depressed. When we bumped into each other now he was smiling and his entire being radiated a sense of joy.

"How did you do it?" I asked him. "You look like an entirely different person. How did you develop the joy I see on you now?"

"When we spoke a number of years ago, you tried to influence me to become a more positive person. You suggested that I make a daily list of at least ten good things that happened to me that day," he said. "I argued that this wouldn't help me. It wasn't my fault I was so unhappy. The root cause was that my parents were to blame. Nobody gave me what I needed to be a happy person. Others were to blame and I was angry at everyone I knew.

"About a year ago, I gave my entire spiel to a tough personal coach. He told me that I was choosing to be unhappy and miserable. I screamed at him, and told him that the way he was talking to me was just making me feel worse. I thought he would back down, like most people I intimidated with my anger. But to my surprise and shock, he spoke to me like no one had spoken to me before.

"'You can go around blaming everyone else,' he said to me. 'But it's your own responsibility to make yourself happy in life. The more you blame others, the less you will do anything to change your pattern of thinking. It's your own pattern of thinking that's destroying your life. Stop it! Stop ruining your life! There's a lot of good in your life that you can be grateful for. Notice it and you will live a joyful life. Continue to willfully blind yourself, and you will be a miserable human being. It's up to you. I can try to help you develop a pattern of gratitude. But only you can do it for yourself. If you keep avoiding seeing what you can be grateful for, that's your decision, and that is what you will keep seeing: Nothing to be grateful for. But if right this moment you fully commit yourself to being a master at noticing what you can be grateful for, you will find things each and every day. Stop acting like an imbecile and start thinking like an intelligent human being.' This was said with such intensity that I was left speechless.

"I was furious at that person. I was looking for sympathy and I didn't get it. I felt awful. Then the next day I said to myself, 'I have to admit that he is right. I do notice what I focus on: negativity. Let's see what happens when I am utterly resolved to see what there is to be grateful for.'

"The next day I noticed a number of things I could be grateful for. And the next day I noticed even more things. And then I noticed even more things. Somehow it was almost like I was living on an entirely different planet.

"I am grateful to that personal coach. He wasn't gentle and he didn't seem to be understanding. But he was wise and he cared about me more than anyone else ever cared about me before. He cared about me so much that he was willing for me to go through a period of time when I was angry at him. He knew that if I changed my focus to a focus on gratitude, I would live a much better life than I had ever dreamed I would. There aren't enough words to describe how grateful I am to him."

4.

Picture How Great You Will Feel When You Master Gratitude

We become motivated to do things when we realize how much we will benefit by doing them. People are willing to do many things that they don't enjoy doing because of the benefits and gain they know will result from what they will do.

We are also motivated to do certain things when we realize how much we will lose out by not doing them. Even thought it might be difficult to do something, we will do it if we feel that we will suffer much more by not doing that thing.

We can utilize this principle of human nature to motivate ourselves to become more grateful. Take, for example, a commitment to read at least a section of this book each day until you have read it five times. There are so many things to do, to study, and to read that it will take effort to reread this book a number of times. If, after one reading of this book, you find yourself mastering gratitude, terrific! But if you see that you really need to implant the thoughts of gratitude into your mind so that you automatically respond with more gratitude, by reading a section daily for five cycles you are much more likely to become a more grateful person.

See yourself being a master of gratitude in the future. Mentally picture how this will help you feel joy the moment you wake and are grateful for being alive. See how you can be grateful and happy for each breath. Realize that when you master gratitude, you will see a happy face every time you look into the mirror. See how your entire quality of life will be improved. See how other people will tell you that they enjoy being around you because you are such a happy person.

If, after realizing how wonderful you will feel after mastering gratitude, you feel wholly motivated to master it, that's great. If you have not yet reached that point, then you can add the following exercise: Visualize how much you will lose out by not being grateful. See a clear picture of how you will be robbing yourself of all the benefits of gratitude. See how much sadder you will be in your life. See how much more irritation and anger you will experience. See how much worse your relationships with others will be. See how much negativity and even misery you will experience in your life. And when you actually picture this and feel it, repeat the positive visualization. See your negativity melting away. See your happiness and joy increasing as you become more and more grateful throughout your life.

Don't just read about this visualization — actually do it. People who are used to mastering positive traits and patterns by utilizing the power of visualization will find this easy to do. There is great pleasure in gaining mastery over positive qualities. But if you aren't yet used to doing similar exercises, it might take special effort to do it. As you see the many benefits, you will build your motivation to put this into practice.

"I used to say that I wasn't a visualizer. I didn't easily make pictures in my mind. And I wasn't able to see myself at a future time. I've spoken to other people I know and I find that some are like me, while others easily visualize any potential positive pattern that they wish. What can I do to increase my ability to visualize?"

Someone asked this question to a person who has taught many people to utilize the mind's power to visualize. He was told, "There are many levels of clarity of people's mental pictures. Everyone sees mental pictures on some level. For example, if I ask you to describe the difference between a giraffe and a zebra, what would you say? Can you see a zebra with its stripes? Can you see a giraffe's long neck? Even if you don't think that you can visualize, if you can describe the difference, it means that you are picturing this on some inner mental level.

"Imagine that you are able to see yourself benefiting from gratitude. Just imagine that you are creating inner mental pictures of the happiness and joy that will be yours when you master gratitude. This will be registering in your inner mind, even if you don't upgrade your ability to visualize."

5.

Self-Image of Being Grateful

*W*ho are you? You have many possible ways of answering. And the way you in fact do answer will have a major impact on your entire life. Self-image refers to your general sense of personal value and worth. Self-image also refers to the specific traits and qualities you believe you have or lack.

View yourself as being a person who is grateful and fervently wants to keep upgrading his level of gratitude. This will lead to more words and acts of gratitude. This is who you are and it is an integral part of what you do.

Some people might challenge this. "If a person is frequently ungrateful, shouldn't he be honest with himself? Isn't it self-deception to think of himself as a person who is grateful? Shouldn't he be saying to himself, "I am an ungrateful person!'?"

For some individuals this might be preferable. They will say to themselves, "Isn't it awful that I am an ungrateful person! I must really improve. I need to make positive changes in my thoughts, words, and actions, and then I can begin to view myself as a grateful person."

But many people are more likely to keep upgrading their attribute of gratitude by having a self-image of being grateful, even though they, like the vast majority of human beings, need to keep increasing their level of gratitude. Seeing themselves as having a fervent wish to be more grateful will lead to more gratitude in action.

One formula for building up a self-image of being grateful is to look at yourself in a mirror twice daily, for an entire month, and say, "You are a grateful person and you have a lot to be grateful for."

Then repeat five times, "I am a grateful person with a lot to be grateful for." "I am a grateful person with a lot to be grateful for." "I am a grateful person with a lot to be grateful for." "I am a grateful person with a lot to be grateful for." "I am a grateful person with a lot to be grateful for."

Those who wish to build up the attribute of patience along with gratitude can spend ten minutes a day for a month repeating to themselves slowly as they breathe slowly and deeply, "I am a grateful person with a lot to be grateful for."

Every grateful statement and action will strengthen your self-image of being a grateful person. This will lead to even more words and actions of gratitude and your positive self-image in this area will become increasingly solidified.

I asked a person who excelled in the trait of gratitude how he had developed it.

"I can't really take credit for it myself," he replied. "I am grateful to my parents for influencing me to view myself as someone who is grateful. When I was a young boy both my father and mother kept reinforcing my view of myself as someone who is grateful. Whenever I thanked them or others for something, they said to me enthusiastically, 'It's wonderful that you are such a grateful boy.'

"I've been told numerous times that I have a strong sense of gratitude. Each time I hear this, I am grateful to my father and mother for what they did to develop this quality that has greatly enhanced my life."

6.

What You Remember Is a Statement About Who You Are

*S*ome people think that when they remember an event, an occurrence, a situation, or a period of time, what they remember is what actually happened.

But the reality is that each event, occurrence, situation, and period of time can be looked at from many perspectives. We can remember what we liked and appreciated, or we can remember what we didn't like and didn't appreciate.

Happy people remember what was positive and how they gained and grew from events, occurrences, situations, and periods of time. Therefore they are happy. And their emotion of happiness influences them to see even more of what was positive and how they gained and grew. Happy people realize that they can mentally relive their grateful moments as often as they choose. So their enormous mental library of the good things that have already happened to them enables them to be grateful for all the past positive things that they have experienced at any time during their lives. Master this, and your own happiness will be greatly increased. People who are consistently sad tend to see what was wrong and what they didn't like. Even when there are events that are clearly positive to most people, some will still focus on the aspects and parts that went wrong and weren't to their liking. This focusing on the negative creates emotional distress. The person experiencing this might think that he is just looking at things as they are. But it's really his own limited focus that is creating this as a negative experience.

Most things that you remember have aspects to be grateful for and aspects that you wished were different. When you keep your focus on what you liked or what is better than it could have been, you will experience gratitude.

Grateful people have many memories of things to be grateful about. An event could have had its challenges, but they remember how grateful they were for the positive aspects of what happened.

People driving to a certain destination might have had a flat tire that got them to where they were going much later than they had planned. A grateful person will always remember how some kind person helped them out, so that eventually they arrived earlier than they would have had that person not come along.

A meal wasn't ready on time, and some of the food was burnt. A grateful person remembers how grateful he is for the meal that he did have and the food that was cooked just right.

People have a multitude of memories from their childhood. A grateful person will have a tremendous amount of grateful memories.

When people remember their vacations, those who have internalized gratitude will remember many things for which to be grateful.

When people remember other people, a grateful person will remember the good things those people did for him.

What you remember of your memories and how you recall them tells you a lot about who you are. Build up the gratitude aspects of your memories and your memories will make the statement that you are a grateful person.

Someone related to me an interesting experience he had had. In the course of a week he spoke to two different men about the yeshivos they had attended. One was full of complaints. He complained about the teachers and he complained about the other students. He complained about the dormitory and he complained about the food. "What did you appreciate there?" he was asked. He replied, "I did appreciate some things. But what stands out strongly in my mind is all the many things that weren't the way they should have been."

The other man was full of gratitude and appreciation for the yeshiva he had attended. He was grateful for all that he had learned from his teachers and the guidance they had given him. He was grateful to the other students with whom he had studied and who were his friends. He was grateful for his dormitory room and was grateful for the cooking staff. "Did you have any complaints?" he was asked. He replied, "Of course, not everything was perfect. But the memories that stand out in my mind are memories of all that I gained and benefited."

These two men seemed to have attended two different institutions. However, they had attended the same yeshiva at the same time. In one way their situations were very similar. In reality, their subjective experiences were entirely different.

7.

"For What Am I Grateful Right Now?"

A question that you can ask yourself any time you wish is, "For what am I grateful right now?"

How will it affect your life if you build up the habit of asking this question to yourself at least ten times a day? The only way that you can know for sure is to actually do it.

The people who have asked themselves this question daily have found that they can always think of something for which to be grateful. Since the question asks you to think of what you are grateful for, your inner mind will look for an answer. And your mind will have gratitude on its consciousness.

Asking, "For what am I grateful right now?" will become a habit for you. It only takes a few seconds to ask. It will only take a few more seconds to answer.

As you are reading this, you can be grateful that you know how to read, that your brain is functioning, and that your mind knows the meaning of these words.

Right now you can be grateful for any of the good things that already happened in your life. Right now you can be grateful for all the knowledge and wisdom that your brain has stored in its magnificent data base. Right now you can be grateful for the fact that there were people who cared for your welfare in the past. Right now you can be grateful for a multitude of things.

As I am writing this, I am grateful for the thought that someone will be reading this and will add more gratitude into their lives. I don't know who specifically will be reading this. Since you are reading this right now, I am grateful to you for doing so. You are helping me help someone enhance his life. Thank you.

A student told me that his father had a habit that used to annoy him. It was a minor habit, but he found it irritating. His father would frequently say, "You know," when he spoke. As politely and respectfully as he could, he had pointed this out to his father. His father told him that he hadn't been aware of this, and he would try to avoid it. But this habit was so entrenched that it wasn't so easy to just stop saying, "You know." As his father would say, "You know, everyone has such habits."

I suggested to the son that whenever his father said, "You know," he should ask himself, "What am I grateful for right now?" Let his father's habit create the habit in his own mind of asking this gratitude-enhancing question.

The son reported to me, "First of all, I have a tremendous amount of things to be grateful for about my father. In a short time, I would think, 'What are you grateful for right now?' whenever I heard anyone say, 'You know.' Now I am even grateful that my father says, 'You know,' since it is has made me a much more grateful person."

8.

Keep a Gratitude Journal

Thinking about gratitude is wonderful. But writing down what you are grateful for in a journal will have a stronger effect.

When you keep a gratitude journal, the process of writing down the things for which you are grateful makes them more concrete. Seeing the items adding up on paper gives you an ever-increasing realization that you have much for which to be grateful.

Some people like to set a minimum specific number of items to add each day. Some add at least three a day. Some add at least five a day. And some write down at least ten a day.

Your resolution to write down a specific number is likely to give you an incentive to find more things for which to be grateful. The higher your quota for each day, the more things you will notice.

Some people are concerned that they won't keep this up. They have started similar projects but stopped after a relatively short time.

Gratitude towards our Father, our King, Creator and Sustainer of the universe, and towards people, is so precious that even if we do this for just a few days, we will have gained greatly from our efforts.

Someone kept a gratitude journal for much longer than he thought he would, and he shared with me: "I felt certain that I wouldn't keep writing in a journal for more than a week. This seemed to me to be too limited a goal, so I wasn't motivated to even start.

"Fortunately for me, a friend insisted that I do this for at least a week. 'Only write down three items a day,' he said. 'This will only take you a few moments and perhaps you will continue longer than you think.'

"He was so insistent that I felt I would save time by agreeing to write down three items a day for a week. This would take up less time than listening to him go on and on about how much I would benefit.

"That was six months ago. This seemingly minor habit had a pervasive influence on my life. I found myself looking for things to be grateful for, and my general level of happiness was much higher than I had anticipated."

9.

Be Grateful for All Your Skills, Talents, and Inner Resources

The Almighty has blessed each of us with our unique mixture of skills, talents, and inner resources. Be grateful to Him for each and every one. This gratitude enables you to maintain humility at the same time as you recognize and appreciate those gifts. Humility does not mean that you deny the gifts you were given. Rather, it means that you have a high level of gratitude.

There are two problems that people might have when it comes to recognizing their skills, talents, and inner resources. On one extreme, there are people who take full credit for what they have been given as natural strengths. This makes them conceited and arrogant. They tend to boast. They tend to see themselves as better than others. This prevents them from learning from others. They need to realize that without the Almighty's assistance, they wouldn't be able to do anything.

On the other extreme, there are people who totally deny their inner strengths. They have feelings of unworthiness and inferiority. They don't believe that they have been given as many strengths as they see others having. They don't believe in themselves — and in a way, that is denying the unlimited abilities of the Creator. He has given every single human being the potential to create his own unique greatness. If one has not yet seen one's own potential, one's highest priority is to find mentors who can help bring it out.

Gratitude for all the positive qualities and strengths that the Almighty has given you will create a spiritual dimension to all of your skills and talents. You recognize them. At the same time, you always keep in mind that they are gifts from your loving Father and powerful King. You appreciate them greatly. You use them for your own welfare and for the welfare of as many of the Creator's children as you can.

With a strong awareness that you are a child of the Creator, your positive self-image and sense of worth is a given. You don't need to prove this to anyone else, nor to yourself. You don't need your skills and talents to claim intrinsic value. You have had unlimited value from the moment you were born, and this stays with you your entire life. This gives you the emotional freedom to enjoy and benefit from the myriad gifts that you were given.

"I heard a talk about being grateful to the Almighty for all of my skills and talents. But I've always considered myself an average person, quite mediocre. My attitude toward myself was that I didn't have any special talents.

"I approached a rabbi who was considered an expert at bringing out the best in people. His basic outlook was that the Almighty gave every human being many strengths. I felt that my situation would be challenging for him. I lacked special skills and talents. What would he be able to find that I wasn't already aware of?

"To my amazement, he began showing me that I was overlooking skills and talents that were really right there once I knew where to look. He started off by asking me what the main things were that I had learned in school. Of course I knew how to read and write. I had taken it for granted. But even before that, I went from not being able to understand even one word in any language, to being an expert at speaking my first language fluently. This is a skill for which I need to be grateful to the Almighty. There were a multitude of words that I knew in more than one language. I knew quite a lot about many subjects. When asked about different topics, I began to see that I knew much more than I had realized.

"He asked me about things that I had done in my life for fun and enjoyment. What hobbies did I have at any time in my life? What things had I watched others do that I could also do? The amount of things that fit into this category was truly impressive. I could hardly believe what I was finding out about myself.

"The person who pointed all these things out to me told me that he is absolutely positive that if I would have a few personal coaches who were knowledgeable about how to show me how to do things that I didn't yet know, the amount of skills and talents that I could gain would be astronomical. He told me about books available from which, if I would need and wish to, I would be able to gain knowledge and information about doing a tremendous amount of things.

"The attitude that the Almighty gave me many skills and talents for me to choose to develop, and that I should be grateful for this, opened up a whole new world for me. I had needlessly limited myself greatly. Knowing that I could continuously add to my inner resources increased my level of gratitude exponentially."

10.

"His Kindness Is Forever."

*T*here is a phrase in Psalms that will transform our lives when we frequently repeat it. The more frequently you say these words and feel it, the more gratitude and joy you will experience in your life.

"His kindness is forever" (*Tehillim* 136:1); in Hebrew, "*ki l'olam chasdo.*" So it is only three words in Hebrew; four words if you say it in English.

How many times a day do you see expressions of the Almighty's kindness? Constantly! Each and every moment that you are alive. Each breath you take. Every word you are able to say. Your ability to take each step. Every bite of food you eat. Every single item you own. Every single item you can use when others permit it. Every instant when your brain works and you can remember anything. Every moment that you enjoy anything, from the smell of fresh bread to hearing a song you like.

Imagine what your day will be like when you realize again and again throughout the day that your loving Father and powerful King, Creator and Sustainer of the universe, is giving you something that is an expression of His kindness to you. We have elaborated on this in *Growth Through Tehillim* (ArtScroll).

What would each day be like if you would make it a regular pattern to repeat this verse at least one hundred times a day? That means you would become more aware of even the smallest kindnesses that the Almighty does for you each and every day.

You don't have to limit yourself to only one hundred times a day. If you utilize this as much as you can, you will find yourself connecting to the Creator throughout the day. Each day will be an adventure in spirituality. Each day will be a happy day. The thoughts in your mind will be appreciation and gratitude. This creates boundless energy that will give deep meaning and pleasure to your entire life.

As you read this section, you will be making a decision. The decision is: "Will I practice saying, 'His kindness is forever' one hundred times a day for a month, or won't I?" Only you can answer this question by what you ultimately do.

Where are you on a scale of one to ten, if one is, "It's not too likely that I will," and ten is, "I will. I am totally committed and have resolved to do this daily at least for a month"? If you are not yet at a ten, what would you need to know that you could gain for it to become a ten? People are willing to invest time and energy into those things that will ultimately benefit them with a joyful, meaningful life. A deep appreciation of this verse will give your life great meaning and joy. Test it out for yourself.

After I suggested to someone that he repeat this verse one hunred times a day, he told me that he gained tremendously from it. And he realized while he was in the process of doing this that he gained greatly by repeating the essence of this verse with a personalization. He would say, "Your kindness to me is forever." Each time, he would spend a moment to realize that he was talking directly to the Creator and Sustainer of the universe Whose love for him was infinite, and thanking Him for the kindness he was receiving. This was tremendously powerful.

11.

Shabbos: a Day of Gratitude

Shabbos is the ultimate day of celebration. Everything else that a person can celebrate in this world is minor and miniscule compared to what we celebrate on Shabbos. On Shabbos we celebrate the creation of the entire universe and everything in it.

This consciousness is enhanced by the Talmudic statement: "A person is obligated to say, 'The world was created for me'" (*Sanhedrin* 37a). So when you celebrate the creation of the world, you are not celebrating something that merely exists out there somewhere. Rather, you are celebrating the universe that is your personal universe, and was created by your loving Father and powerful King, the Creator and Sustainer of all that exists.

On Shabbos, a day of peace and serenity, your mind is free; it is a time to reflect on all that you are grateful for. You benefit regularly from some things in the world. And there are many things you benefit from once in a while. Regardless of whether you have benefited from some of the things in the world in the past, or you will be able to benefit from some of these things in the future, you can be grateful for them each and every Shabbos.

When you associate Shabbos with gratitude, everything that you do to prepare for Shabbos will be done with an underlying theme of gratitude. This will make the entire process of Shabbos cleaning and all the many things that one does in honor of Shabbos much more enjoyable. It is part of your personal celebration of your immense universe.

In order to make this an automatic association, repeat to yourself many times, "Shabbos is my special day of gratitude for all that the Creator has given me."

"I used to find preparing for Shabbos a source of pressure and stress," the mother of a large family related. "I remember how nervous my mother was when she had a lot of things to do. And I thought that this was an automatic reaction that is common to all people.

"The Shabbos meals used to be a time for the children to be rowdy and misbehave. My husband and I insisted that the children behave better, but they often didn't listen as they should.

"An older relative of mine was a guest at our home one Shabbos. Before she left, she called me aside and said to me, 'First of all, I am grateful for a wonderful Shabbos. I appreciate how careful you and your family are to make sure that Shabbos is so special in your home. But I would like to leave you with a Shabbos gift.

"'Shabbos is a day of being grateful for the entire creation and everything that Hashem has given you. When you prepare for Shabbos, let your uppermost thoughts be on gratitude. With everything you do for Shabbos, repeat to yourself, "I am grateful that I have food to cook and prepare. I am grateful for my house to clean. I am grateful for my precious children."

"'And I would like to leave you with a suggestion that I have seen a number of people do. At their Shabbos table, they go around the room and ask everyone, "What are you grateful for?" Then two more times: "What else?"'

"I followed through on this suggestion and it has transformed and elevated my entire Shabbos immensely. I am extremely grateful to my relative for pointing out how I could enlighten my Shabbos with gratitude."

12.

Gratitude for Your Memory and Brain

"*I* am grateful for my memory." How often do you hear people saying this? Do you hear this more frequently or do you hear something like, "I can't remember. I'm always forgetting things. My memory isn't what I would like it to be."

After people read this section, I hope they will develop the habit of consistently being grateful for what they do remember. And they will express this gratitude so frequently that others will also develop the habit of expressing gratitude for their memory. And many more people will hear those people expressing this gratitude, and they too will express their gratitude.

Our brains are amazing. In such a small area we have an ultra-gigantic amount of storage room for the scenes and pictures we have seen in our lives. In our brain's storage we have all the information and ideas we have read and heard.

The present estimate is that we have at least 100 billion neurons (brain cells). Each neuron can store a million bits. The potential in your brain is beyond your comprehension. Be grateful to the Creator for giving it to you as a gift.

Regardless of how much you can't easily recall at will, you still can recall a tremendous amount. We all can recognize much more information when we hear or see it again even if we can't easily recall it on our own. Even people who claim that they can't remember stories or jokes usually remember having heard them when they are repeated. When you learn to improve your ability to recall, you will realize more of your potential and have more to be grateful for.

Do you recognize your own house? That means your memory is working. People with severe memory loss can't even remember this.

Even if you feel that you can't remember people's names or faces, there are a multitude of names and faces that you do remember. Be grateful for each one.

Be grateful for all the information you know. That means that this information is stored in your brain and you have the ability to recall it.

When you increase your gratitude for your memory and brain, you are likely to improve your memory. Your belief in your ability to remember opens up possibilities. Conversely, if someone keeps repeating that he has a poor memory and doesn't remember things, this negative self-programming prevents his memory from working as well as it could. This is especially so because at times we need patience to recall information. If we believe that we can't remember, we don't have the patience to give our brains the time necessary to recall what we want to recall. We all have had the experience of not remembering something at first and then, when we are calm, the memory simply pops into our minds. Be grateful for each such experience.

Your ability to recall what you have stored in your brain works at its optimal best when you are completely calm and relaxed. If you feel tense when you are trying to remember something, breathe slowly and deeply to release tension. Be grateful for each breath. This process will enable you to remember more and think better.

Someone who believed that he had a poor memory spoke to his rabbi and asked what to do to improve his memory. The rabbi shared with him a number of tools and techniques that he could use. The tool that helped this fellow the most was, "Whenever you find it difficult to remember something that you want to remember, ask yourself, 'What ten things do I remember now about anything?' After you see that you do remember ten things, express your appreciation to our Creator for giving you a brain and a memory. In the merit of expressing your gratitude, the Almighty will help you remember even more things. And when you remember to use this tool, be grateful that you remembered it."

13.

Blessings Before and After Eating

The formal blessings (*berachos*) we make before and after we eat are exercises in expressing our gratitude to our Creator for the food He gives us.

After saying these blessing many times, it is easy to just say them routinely. We might say the words exactly as they should be said, but our minds and hearts might not be involved in what we are saying. Saying the blessings are valuable. Even if we don't say them with the focus and concentration that we should, we are still expressing our gratitude on some basic level. But a major ingredient in the purpose of the blessings is missing.

The goal of each and every blessing we make is for us to increase our level of gratitude to our Creator. It helps to say in your own words before a blessing, "Now I am going to express my personal gratitude to my loving Father and powerful King, Creator and Sustainer of the universe, for His kindness to me."

Making a specific announcement that you are grateful for the food the Creator has given you, and that you are now going to express your gratitude, elevates the spiritual level of the physical experience of eating. You are connecting with Hashem, Who loves you more than you love yourself (as the Chofetz Chaim writes in *Sefer Shemiras HaLashon*).

Someone who wanted to improve his level of reciting blessings with *kavanah* (mindfulness) asked what he could do about it.

He was advised, "Make it a minimal goal to recite five blessings a day with a previous statement in your own words that you are grateful for the food you are about to eat, and afterwards that you are grateful for the food you've already eaten. It's worthwhile to mark this off on a piece of paper."

"But isn't five times insufficient?" the fellow asked.

"If your goal is perfection, you are likely to feel overwhelmed at first. Start off with just five times. Then it's much more likely that you will follow through on this goal. Doing this five times a day will build up the habit of having a real sense of gratitude. By doing so, there is a strong likelihood that you will eventually increase the amount of times that you truly feel grateful."

14.

Gratitude for Being Alive

The most precious thing you have is your life. Since you are reading this, it's obvious that you are alive right this moment. And therefore you have the number one thing that can fill you with gratitude.

"But my quality of life isn't what I want it to be!" is the thought that prevents many people from experiencing the joy of being alive and the feelings of gratitude for life.

Wanting the quality of your life to be better and taking positive action to make this happen is no contradiction to being grateful for the precious gift of life. This way you have an inner feeling of joy for being alive, and this positive energy will give you more inner strength to create the kind of life that would be better for you.

The first thing we say when we wake up in the morning is the one-line statement that we are grateful for being alive; in Hebrew, it is *Modeh ani...* That's amazing, isn't it? The first words we utter each day say that we are grateful. This sets the tone for the entire day. "Today I will be grateful from the moment I wake up."

Throughout the day, say with enthusiasm, "I am grateful I am alive!"

"But what if I don't actually feel this way? It's a nice thought and I should be grateful that I am alive, but that's not the way I feel," is a common statement.

The solution to this is to follow the famous advice of Rabbi Moshe Chaim Luzzatto in *Mesilas Yesharim*, chapter seven: "Act externally as if you were enthusiastic, and you will increase your inner feelings of enthusiasm."

Right now you can practice this. Repeat over and over again with enthusiasm, "I am grateful I am alive!"

"I used to be full of frustration and easily became angry," someone told me. "Then one piece of advice totally changed my emotional quality of life. When I think about it now, it seems to me to be so simple that I find it difficult to believe that such an easy practice could make such a major difference.

"My most frequent thoughts throughout the day used to be, 'I feel frustrated that things aren't going the way that I want them to.' I would repeat variations of this theme again and again. They were so automatic for me that I didn't even realize that this was happening in my mind. But the feelings that I would regularly experience were feelings of frustration and anger.

"I asked a rabbi what to do to improve my character traits. He told me that he will give me a powerful formula, but it will only work for me if I repeat it enough times. 'This won't be difficult,' he said, 'but it will take a strong resolution. It won't work if you don't actually repeat it.'

"At first I thought that he might suggest some kabbalistic incantation. And I was a bit disappointed when he told me the formula.

"'Each and every day for at least one month, repeat at least one hundred times, "I am tremendously grateful I am alive."

"'Don't just repeat this in one session. That would be very good to do, but it's not sufficient. At different moments throughout the day, say with enthusiasm, "I am grateful I am alive."

"'Whenever you begin to feel frustrated, immediately say five times with enthusiasm, "I am tremendously grateful I am alive. I am tremendously grateful I am alive. I am tremendously grateful I am alive. I am tremendously grateful I am alive. I am tremendously grateful I am alive."

"'When you keep this up, the onset of your feelings of frustration will be replaced with the positive thoughts and feelings of gratitude.'

"This changed my life."

15.

Drinking Water Gratefully

*T*hinking about gratitude when I was drinking water, I realized that drinking water slowly and repeating to yourself, "I am grateful for this water," creates a wonderful experience.

Before we drink the water, we make the formal blessing over water. In this blessing we acknowledge that Hashem is the "King of the universe" and that everything that exists in the world is because of "His word." We realize that the water we are now drinking is a gift to us from the Creator of it all. And not only is He the Creator of everything, He is the Creator of this water that we are about to drink.

Then, as you drink the water, drink it very, very slowly. And as you are drinking the water slowly, keep repeating in your mind, "I am grateful for this water. I am grateful for this water. I am grateful for this water."

By repeating this each day as you drink water, this becomes an automatic mindset and thought process. You will be increasing gratitude every time you drink water. Your inner brain will associate drinking water with being grateful. Each time you do this, your emotional state will be one of gratitude. This will melt away any distressful or toxic states. And your entire mind/body will be in a positive state of gratitude.

Don't just think to yourself, "This sounds like a good idea." Take action. If it's possible for you right now, get a glass of water and repeat, "I am grateful for this water," as you drink it. If you are not able to drink water right now, mentally think of a specific time when you will apply this.

As we have written many times, your mental state depends on the thoughts that you are thinking at any given moment. So if you find yourself stressed, frustrated, irritated, angry, or in any other distressful emotional state, choose gratitude instead. By going to get a glass of water and slowly drinking it with thoughts of gratitude, you will find yourself in a better state.

Someone said, "Not too long ago, my doctor told me that I was taking in too much sugar. If I wouldn't decrease the amount of sugar I was ingesting, I was in danger of developing a serious health problem. I loved drinking soft drinks and I was sort of addicted to them. How could I cut down on soda and other sugary beverages? I wanted to be careful with my health, but this seemed like a major deprivation. I wasn't certain if I would be able to follow through consistently enough.

"Then it was suggested to me to mentally sweeten plain water with thoughts of gratitude. I could imagine that I was in a desert and didn't have water for two days. Then I miraculously met someone with a bottle of water, and this was the best-tasting water that I had ever drunk. This power of imagination has made it easier for me to see that I can build up my appreciation and gratitude for water. The fact that I have water regularly doesn't mean that I should lower my appreciation and gratitude."

16.

Don't Take Things for Granted

*I*t's easy to lack gratitude because human nature is to take things for granted when we get used to having them. To master gratitude, we need to stop taking things for granted and to increase our thoughts of appreciation.

If someone keeps doing positive things for us regularly, our level of appreciation can lessen. We expect it. Now, we are more likely to notice what that person doesn't do rather than being grateful for what he does do.

The Creator keeps bestowing His tremendous kindnesses on us each and every day when we are awake and when we are asleep, whether we are aware of them or not. There are so many things in our lives that we take for granted.

As an exercise, choose a day on which you will not take anything for granted. Look at everything as if it were new. Look at everything as if this were the first time that this positive thing is happening. Look at all the things you own as if you had just bought or received them today. Look at what you have as if it were invented recently and you are one of the first people on the planet to get it.

This exercise will help you experience what it's like to not take things for granted. It will refresh the newness of what you have and what others are doing for you. You might find this exercise so beneficial that you will want to do it at regular intervals.

A student told me, "When it was suggested that I go for an entire day without taking anything for granted, I thought of making a list of what I have and what others have done for me that I have taken for granted. I felt that this would be easier for me than to imagine that things that aren't new are new.

"I gave the list the title, 'What I take for granted.' In a very short time, the list became longer than I thought it would. Imaginative exercises don't work very well for me, so I didn't think that I could now look at each item on the list as if it were new. But I did think of changing the title of the list. I now wrote on the top of the list, 'Things I can be grateful for.' This worked for me. Just seeing what a long list I have to be grateful for added to my sense of gratitude."

17.

All Gratitude Is Ultimately Gratitude to Our Creator

"*K*indness builds the world" (*Tehillim* 89:3). The Creator created our world in a way that we all need kindness. Without kindness we would not be able to exist in this world. Each time we do an act of kindness we are doing our part to maintain the world. Gratitude for each kindness we receive is an awareness and appreciation for all the goodness that we experience. And the ultimate good in the world is our loving Creator. Awareness of this good means feeling gratitude.

Someone does a minor favor for you. Someone helps you carry a heavy package a short distance. Someone lends you a small amount of money so you can finish paying for something that you bought, as you have slightly less money with you than you need. Someone shows you where a certain building is. Someone points out to you that you accidentally dropped something. You say, "Thank you." When you reflect on what has just happened, you realize that your loving Father and powerful King, Creator and Sustainer of the universe, has just sent you His messenger and agent to be kind to you. It's a small step for a member of the human race. But after taking a more comprehensive look at what has happened, you realize that you have received yet another lesson in the infinite and eternal kindness of our Creator. Your gratitude puts you in touch with this.

When you look at each person who says or does anything kind to you as the Creator's agent, you look at this person in a more elevated and spiritual way. Even a long time after this seemingly minor event happened, you can still remember that the kind person has served as the Almighty's agent. His stature has been raised in your eyes. And when you continually view other people this way, they will respond to you in a higher way. This entire process is a step forward in raising the spiritual level of the world, and it started from just a few words or an easy-to-do action.

"I feel that I am missing spirituality in my life," a forty-year-old businessman complained. "A good part of the day I am involved in purely material matters."

"Find the spiritual in the material," he was told. "Do you have opportunities to be kind to others in some way each and every day?"

"Quite frequently," he replied. "And I'm certain that if I keep my mind focused on searching for more opportunities, I will find them."

"And do you have opportunities to thank people for things that they do for you?"

"Again, quite frequently."

"Each time you thank a person for doing something for you, even a minor thing, add a mental 'thank you' to our Creator. This will give each and every day many spiritual moments."

After applying this advice, the man felt that his life underwent a major transformation; it was infused with more spirituality.

18.

Grateful to Our Creator

"*I* am grateful to my Creator."

Repeat this sentence out loud: "I am grateful to my Creator."

Repeat it over and over again until you feel it.

This is one of the most important messages you can tell yourself.

Living with this gratitude elevates your entire life. You become a more spiritual person. You become a more joyful person. You become a kinder and more compassionate person. You become a calmer and more peaceful person. You become a person who lives in greater harmony with others.

If you won't be grateful to your Creator Who has created the entire world and everything in it, then to whom will you be grateful?

If you won't be grateful to your Creator, you are missing the entire purpose of life. He has created the world for your benefit.

"A person is obligated to say, 'The world was created for me' (*Sanhedrin* 37a). Everything that has kept you alive until now comes from Him. All the good in your life comes from Him.

Right this moment, imagine the joy you would feel if you were to experience an intense feeling of gratitude to your Creator.

I told a group of people to repeat, "I am grateful to my Creator" five minutes each day for a month.

Some of the results:

"At first, I found it difficult to keep this up. This gave me a jolt. The Creator is giving me life each moment of each day and He gives me the air I breathe. Why is it so hard for me to express my gratitude? This self-rebuke gave me a strong feeling of motivation. I was committed to using the power of repeating messages to myself to build up this gratitude."

"I realized that I would only be able to repeat this for five minutes at a time if I would sing it with a tune. So I would sing this five minutes each day. It became my favorite song."

"The first day when I heard this, I found myself having to wait for something to start. I began to feel frustrated. Then I said to myself, 'This is a perfect time to repeat, "I am grateful to my Creator" for five minutes.' It totally transformed the waiting into an uplifting experience. Throughout the month, I chose potentially frustrating moments to practice this. After a while, the stirrings of feelings of frustration became a trigger to begin my exercise."

"Someone saw me smiling while I was waiting in line at my local supermarket. He asked me if anything special is going on in my life. 'There are a lot of special things that I'm beginning to become more aware of,' I replied."

"By repeating, 'I am grateful to my Creator,' I began to realize that everyone who is kind to me in any way was sent to me by my Creator. I increased my gratitude towards those people and I increased my gratitude to the Creator of it all."

19.

"Next!" to Gratitude

*O*ur stream of thought keeps flowing like a mighty river. We constantly think one thought after another. At any given moment we can consciously choose to think a grateful thought. This miraculous ability is one of the greatest gifts we've been given: The ability to select gratitude this very moment.

If you ever find your stream of thought needlessly having negative and counterproductive content, say, "NEXT!" Then select a thought of gratitude.

"NEXT! to Gratitude." Repeat this with a joyful tone of voice again and again. Let your voice sound as joyful as can be. "NEXT! to Gratitude. NEXT! to Gratitude."

Then, whenever you want to choose gratitude as your theme of thought, all you have to do is say: "NEXT! to Gratitude."

What if this doesn't work for you? Then say with all your heart and all your soul in a loud, clear voice, "I hereby declare that I am going to choose a thought of gratitude. I am alive now and I'm grateful for it." As long as you say these words, you are choosing a grateful thought.

"But I can't just choose to think of gratitude!" you might protest. If you do think this, let me ask you a question. Did you read the first sentence of this paragraph? If you did, it means that your mind focused its attention on that sentence, didn't it? Obviously, yes. Then it's just as obvious that you can choose to focus your attention on the next sentence. And that is: "I will think of gratitude so much that it will get easier and easier." Even if you say to yourself right now, "I don't know for sure that I will think of gratitude to that extent," it still shows that you were able to place your attention on what you read. As you keep doing that with the rest of this book, little by little the thoughts about gratitude will be integrated and you will find yourself a more grateful person.

"I am an obsessive type of guy," someone said to me.

"Do you choose to be obsessive on the negative or on the positive?" I asked him.

"I don't choose," he replied. "The thoughts come on their own. And most of them are negative."

"If you could choose your thoughts, would you want to choose gratitude?" I asked him.

"Of course I would," he said.

"So right now please say, 'I choose to think of being grateful for being able to speak.'"

He repeated this.

"So this proves that when you decide to choose a gratitude sentence, you can actually choose it."

"But this will take a lot of effort," he challenged.

"I fully agree with you. So you have a choice: to do what's simple and easy, to keep making yourself miserable by allowing your negative, obsessive thoughts to ruin your life, or you can make the effort to consistently choose thoughts of gratitude. Not only will you gain from the gratitude thoughts, you will also feel a tremendous feeling of accomplishment that you were able to achieve something that is difficult to do."

The smile on his face showed that he agreed with this way of looking at it.

20.

Focusing on Those with More or with Less

*H*ow we judge what we have will be a major factor in whether we will be grateful or not.

If someone focuses on those with more, it's easy to lack gratitude for what one has. "They have a lot more than I do. What I have doesn't seem to be very much. Therefore, I lack gratitude." This is a thought pattern that creates ingratitude.

If someone focuses on those with less, it is easy to feel grateful for what one has. "Compared to them, I have a lot."

Whenever you feel that it's difficult for you to be grateful because you would like more than you now have, or would like for your life situation to be better than it is, focus on other people on our planet who have less than you. Or direct your focus on people whose life situation is worse than yours. There are always people who have less than you, and there are always people who have more challenging life situations.

All you need to do is find a person who has much less than you and is still grateful for what he has, and you will have a role model from whom to learn. Similarly, look for a person whose life is extremely challenging and is still happy and grateful for what he does have.

If, regardless of how hard you look, you can't find anyone with less than you who is still full of gratitude for what he has, then you can be such a master of gratitude that your attitude of gratitude will be a role model for others. And you can be grateful for this opportunity to enhance the lives of others.

The ideal would be to feel so grateful for what one does have that one doesn't focus at all on what others have. "As long as I have something for which to be grateful, I will be grateful. And there is always something to be grateful."

A few years ago a person who would be considered successful by most people's standards shared with me, "Looking back at my childhood, a thought pattern that I remember having is, 'He has more than me.' 'His birthday present was better than mine.' 'He gets to travel to more interesting places.' 'He is luckier than I am.' 'He has more friends.' 'He lives in a nicer house.'

"On my fortieth birthday I made a mental accounting of my life. I thought about various traits and patterns that I had. The most distressful part of this mental accounting was that I noticed I wasn't very happy in my life. When I asked myself why, and thought about it, I realized that I kept feeling that I had less than others. I was told to look back at my childhood for this pattern, and that's when I realized how often this theme had come. There were many ways that others had it better than I did. And my mind was full not only of thoughts of having less, but of being less.

"I realized that if I wanted to live the rest of my life joyfully, I needed to do one of two things. Either I could make it my goal to be so successful in every way that is important to me that I would be far ahead of everyone I knew, so I would find it easier to be grateful for my accomplishments, successes, and possessions — or I could learn to gain greater mastery over my thoughts. I would choose to think thoughts of gratitude as my automatic way of thinking. The first choice would take so much time, effort, and energy that I would be in a constant, frustrating race with others. I might never reach my goal, and even if I did reach it, it was certainly not going to last. Eventually someone would pass me by. This way of thinking would give me many years of stress and frustration, and there really wasn't a way that this would give me gratitude and happiness. It was obvious that the wiser approach would be to be grateful for what I had. Choosing this pattern of thought was one of the best choices I have made in my life."

21.

Reminders to Be Grateful

The Almighty sends us constant reminders to be grateful. Whenever we see someone who is lacking something important that we ourselves have, we have yet another reminder to be grateful.

While our first reaction should be compassion and caring, the next thought should be a sense of gratitude for what we do have. And this thought can increase our compassion and empathy for the other person's situation.

Seeing someone who needs a wheelchair serves as a reminder that you should appreciate being able to walk on your own two feet, while a person who needs a wheelchair will have a multitude of other things for which to be grateful.

Moreover, there is no wheelchair club to which one is either a member or not. Rather, anyone might find himself in a situation where, either temporarily or permanently, he needs one himself.

As long as he can walk on his own, he can appreciate that now, in the present, he is able to walk.

Seeing someone who is blind serves as a reminder that you can appreciate being able to see. Someone who is blind will have a multitude of other things for which to be grateful.

Seeing someone begging for money serves as a reminder that you can appreciate that you are in a better financial situation. Someone who begs for money will still have a multitude of other things for which to be grateful.

Seeing someone who has an illness serves as a reminder that you can appreciate your own health in this area. Someone who is ill can be grateful for the years when he had good health, but while in the present he will still have a multitude of things for which to be grateful.

Seeing an elderly person who is frail and weak serves as a reminder that you can appreciate your energy and vitality. And someone who is now frail and weak can be grateful for the past, when he used to have energy and vitality, and can still find a multitude of other things for which to be grateful.

Seeing someone who is pessimistic and kvetchy serves as a reminder that you can appreciate having a more optimistic and grateful approach to life. Someone who is pessimistic and kvetchy might have a multitude of things for which to be grateful, but he needs to turn the channel of his mind from the kvetchy station to the gratitude station. He can do this the instant he chooses to do so.

Be very careful not to say something insensitive to a person who is missing something that you have. At times this is so obvious that it should not have to be stated; for example, someone who is happily married should not say to a friend who is single, "Every time I see you, I think of how grateful I am that I am married." A person with a well-paying job should not tell someone who has lost his job, "When I think of you, I have a greater appreciation for my job."

If someone actually says something similar, it would give the recipient of the comment a chance to say, "When I hear you say this, I increase my gratitude for having been blessed with more *seichel* (common sense)."

When traveling to work each morning I would complain about how slowly the traffic was moving. Invariably I would arrive at work in a highly irritable state of mind. Right off the main street was a major hospital. I knew it was there, but didn't give it very much thought. One day, fairly close to the hospital, I witnessed the aftermath of a major car crash. Ambulances rushed the injured to the hospital. It hit me then that each time I pass the hospital I should gain a greater sense of gratitude for my good health. This had a very positive effect on my daily state of mind. I arrived at work feeling much better than I used to feel.

22.

"I Am Full of Gratitude Today"

I would like to suggest an exercise for a day when you feel adventurous enough to try it. For an entire day, whenever asked how you are, respond with, "I am full of gratitude today."

You might even say, "I am full of gratitude today" to someone who didn't ask you how you are.

The first thought that usually goes through the other person's mind is, "What special thing happened today?"

This gives you an opportunity to think about what happened that was special that day. Each and every day there is always something special for which to be grateful. The one factor that always exists is that on this day you are alive. By virtue of being alive today, today is special and you are entitled to be full of gratitude today.

Some people respond, "But how can I say that I am full of gratitude today if I'm not full of gratitude today?" And the question to ask these responders is, "And why aren't you full of gratitude today?" You, like every live human being, have much for which to be grateful. It's merely a question of whether we are in touch with those factors. So instead of refraining from saying, "I am full of gratitude today" because you don't truly feel that way, do the opposite.

Think about some of the many things you could be grateful for today if you were to honestly and sincerely say, "I am full of gratitude today."

And if someone develops the habit of usually saying, "I am full of gratitude today," if one day he doesn't say this, others will remind him, "If you wanted to say, 'I am full of gratitude today,' what could you be grateful for today?"

"When it was suggested to me to tell everyone I spoke to today, 'I am full of gratitude today,' I felt that this would sound strange. I didn't feel comfortable saying this. It didn't seem true. I wasn't really full of gratitude. The reality was that I was often a bit negative and pessimistic. And when I thought about how negative and pessimistic I was, I felt even worse.

"I asked a Torah scholar if it was permissible for me to state that I was full of gratitude even though I wasn't. He smiled and said to me, 'We all have many reasons to be full of gratitude, even when we are facing challenges. Since, when you speak this way, it will become how you feel, I suggest that you try this out and see how it affects you.'

"You can't imagine how difficult it was for me to say, 'I am full of gratitude today,' to anyone else. I decided to begin by saying this to myself. Throughout the day I would repeat to myself, 'I am full of gratitude today.' The next words that I thought were, 'Sure you are. Tell it to the Marines!' This made me smile. I remembered two different people who used this expression. Then I felt a little better and remembered what I was grateful for. I kept this up for over a month. This was becoming a habit and it grew easier and easier for me to remember to be grateful.

"I remember the day when I said to someone else, 'I am full of gratitude today.' It was a day that didn't seem special. But it was. It was the day that I realized that I was becoming a much more grateful person than I used to be. I was grateful for developing more gratitude."

23.

Gratitude for Life's Challenges

*W*hen things go well in our life, it's relatively easy to be grateful for the good that we experience. But what about when life is challenging? What about adversity? What about the difficulties that we experience? Am I trying to claim that it's easy to be grateful for the challenges, difficulties, and adversity that occurs in life?

No, I'm not trying to claim that it's easy. It's hard to cope with challenges, difficulties, and adversity. And it's even more difficult to experience gratitude in these situations. But it's humanly possible. When we realize that all that happens to us is for our ultimate benefit and that everything that occurs is meaningful and planned, we gain an awareness that there is something for which to be grateful. Remember, "This, too, is for the best."

The Almighty helps us develop our character with the tests He sends us. Developing our character is an essential aspect of our purpose and goal in life. Therefore everything that helps us develop our character is something for which we can be grateful.

"This, too, will help me develop my character." This is the motto that should be with us our entire life. Each and every day we have opportunities to develop our character. Each and every experience in our life is an opportunity to develop our character. Keeping our focus on how we can elevate ourselves and refine our attributes gives us a broader perspective on all that occurs.

The more we grow and develop from the challenges that we face, the more we will be able to experience gratitude when we see how much we've gained and grown.

A middle-aged man who had a consistently sad look on his face attended a class on happiness. He challenged the rabbi who spoke about being grateful for the good in our lives: "That's fine and well for younger people who have hope for a good life of abundance and accomplishment. They have a lot to look forward to. They have their health and have the energy to accomplish things. But what about someone whose life is closer to the end than to the beginning? What about a person who faces daily challenges?"

The rabbi responded, "How have you developed as a person from the difficulties that you've experienced in life? How have you developed into a more mature person and a deeper thinker because of your challenges? How have you gained from what you've experienced that you wouldn't have gained if you would have had an easy life of leisure?"

The person said that his intellectual understanding of the purpose of life is much more profound and comprehensive than if he would have had an easy life. He has gained much wisdom from his life experiences. He has realized that our purpose in this world is not just to live a superficial life of pleasure. Life has a spiritual dimension that is, in truth, the purpose of our lives.

"Are you grateful for having gained this wisdom and depth?"

"I certainly am," he replied.

"That is what is meant by being grateful for challenges. It's not that you wanted to suffer, but that you are grateful for what you've gained spiritually and intellectually."

"This does make sense to me," the man acknowledged.

24.

Be Grateful It's Better than it Might Have Been

We evaluate every situation in our own mind and thoughts. Those that we evaluate as positive, we feel good about. Those that we evaluate as negative, we feel bad about. The more positively we evaluate a given situation, the happier and more joyful we feel. The more negatively we evaluate a situation, the more distressed we feel.

Even if a situation or occurrence is not what we would have wanted, if it's better than it might have been, we can be grateful for that. A person who consistently thinks this way will automatically find ways that the situation has positive aspects to it. This will decrease the distress felt when situations and occurrences are challenging. There is often a feeling of relief. Sometimes, a person will actually feel happy about the entire picture.

Be careful about telling someone else who is in pain or distress that a situation is better than it might have been. Depending on how much suffering the person is experiencing, this might not be helpful. Before saying this to someone, think whether it is likely to be beneficial or not. Many people would prefer empathy and compassion, rather than hearing that things are not so bad. Showing sincere concern would be the right thing to say. Minimizing the negativity would not.

Many situations that we felt bad about in the past seemed very negative to us when we first experienced them. But after time passed, we easily saw how we had exaggerated the negative. In our mind, we built up the negative way out of proportion. We discounted all the many positive things in our life in the context of which this loss or disappointment is trivial. Now we can realize that we can be grateful for a tremendous amount of things. Our gratitude gives us a general feeling of well-being. These positive feelings help us cope better with any challenge we face. Our minds work better and it will be easier to find solutions.

I met someone who had been very wealthy but through a number of setbacks had lost his fortune. He was a very happy person and he was consistently grateful for all the good in his life.

"What's your secret?" I asked him. "It would be very easy for someone in your situation to be miserable a good part of the time. Your life seems tough. You have financial pressures that you didn't have before, and you are limited in what you can buy."

"I grew up in a home where the motto of our family was, 'Let's think of all that we can be grateful for.' I was grateful for my wealth when I had it. And now I am more grateful than ever for my health. I am grateful for the home that I have to live in. I am grateful for the food that I am able to provide for my family. Each day I have a multitude of things to be grateful for."

"Would you consider this an example of, 'It's better than it might have been'?"

"It's much better than that. I don't need wealth to have things to be grateful for. My mind is so full of appreciation that I have all the emotional benefits that wealth could possibly give me."

25.

Recognizing What We Had After We Lost It

After we lose something, it's much easier for us to realize the value of what we previously had. We think now, "If only I would have known how good my situation was before, I would have been much more grateful."

Feeling bad about not being grateful for what we had before can cause our thoughts to travel down one of two paths. One is the path of sadness and emotional distress: "Why wasn't I grateful before? It's too bad that now it's too late. I missed out on such an opportunity before. My lack of gratitude is such a problem in my life. And now I have even less than before to be grateful for."

However, it's more productive to think, "I should have been more grateful before. Now I don't have what I had before, but I still have a tremendous amount to be grateful for. Let me learn from my previous lack of gratitude, to be grateful now in the present for all that I can be grateful for."

The second path is a path that will add to our happiness, appreciation, and gratitude in life. This is the path that we would be wise to choose.

I met an elderly person who lived alone and had many physical problems and financial challenges, yet he was highly upbeat and happy. I wondered how he was able to experience such positive emotions despite the difficulties he faced. I asked him about his life experiences and the most important lessons he had learned about life that I could share with others.

A key point that he shared with me was, "When something goes well for you, be grateful for it for the rest of your life. I had a happy childhood. My childhood was happy no matter what else happened to me later on. For my entire life I can be grateful for the many things I enjoyed when I was growing up. I can be grateful for all the positive memories my late wife gave me. I can be grateful for the good things that people did for me throughout my life. Some of the people I am grateful towards are no longer alive. But my feelings of gratitude towards them remain."

"But isn't it difficult to keep on feeling grateful for what is no longer here?" I asked him.

"No. Once this becomes your habitual way of thinking, it's automatic. It's not hard at all. I've met people who are angry and resentful towards people who are no longer alive. It makes a lot more sense to keep up the positive quality of being grateful."

26.

An Hour of Gratitude

*T*here is a powerful exercise that will greatly help you upgrade your level of gratitude. Designate an hour a day to be your hour of gratitude. During this hour, keep your focus on gratitude.

Isn't an hour a long time to do this? Yes, it is. But when you do this exercise for a month, you will find the benefits so great that you will feel that the effort to keep it up for an hour a day is tremendously worthwhile.

And what about spending an hour a day thinking about what you don't like, what makes you unhappy, what makes you resentful, what makes you envious, what you find frustrating, what's not happening that you want to happen, what might go wrong in the future (also known as worrying), what has already gone wrong in the past – isn't an hour a long time to spend on thinking these thoughts? Yes, it is. And many people would find it a great blessing to only think these thoughts for just one hour a day, and for the rest of the day think more pleasant, enjoyable, beneficial, growth-oriented thoughts. Making a resolution to designate an hour a day reserved for thoughts of gratitude will make it easier for you to overcome a tendency to think thoughts that create stress and distress.

"But I don't have that many things to be grateful for," some people might argue. "You would be surprised!" is the answer. Try it out and you will find that you have much more for which to be grateful than you previously imagined.

If you go to a store to buy something, be grateful that the store is there. Be grateful that you have the money to buy what you want to buy, or that someone is willing to lend you the money, or that a store is willing to give you credit.

If you meet someone you know, be grateful that you have people who are friendly towards you.

If the telephone rings, be grateful that you can hear.

If you see anything, be grateful that you can see.

If you have food to eat, be grateful for that food.

If you read something, be grateful that your brain is functioning and you know how to read.

If you smile to yourself in a mirror, be grateful that you have the positive feedback that will help you master positive states.

If you begin to feel irritated or upset over something and remember that this is your hour of gratitude, be grateful that your memory is working and that you have things for which to be grateful and that you can access a state of gratitude rather than an unpleasant one.

If someone else needlessly makes a negative comment, you can say, "This is my hour of gratitude, and I would be very grateful to you if you could point out some things we can be grateful for during this hour."

The following was the reaction of someone who was very excited about the idea of having an hour of gratitude: "I was thrilled to hear about this. I could immediately tell that this was going to be something very meaningful and important in my life. I already had made a conscious effort to work on increasing my level of gratitude, but it was done in a random and disorganized way. The idea of concentrating my focus on gratitude was what I needed.

"I had a tendency to worry. During my hour of gratitude, I was so full of good feelings that any thoughts of worry were very fleeting. My stream of thought just let any worrisome thoughts dissipate. When I thought about something practical I had to take care of, I took care of it in a very efficient and effective manner. But I wasn't going to waste my precious hour of gratitude time counterproductively spent on needless distress-causing thoughts. And when I thought of this, I realized that all the time we are alive is time that we should spend on being grateful to our Creator for the good in our lives. I wasn't going to waste my hour of gratitude, and this became a lesson not to waste my lifetime of gratitude on needless counterproductive thinking."

27.

Gratitude for When Things Do Work Well

Things don't always work the way we would like. Machines break down. People don't remember to do what they said they would. Stores run out of things, and sometimes they are closed when they are scheduled to be open. Letters we are supposed to receive aren't always delivered on time. Messages are not always given to us. The amount of things that don't work out the way they usually do is enormous.

What will your emotional reaction be towards these types of occurrences? It's up to you.

Some people choose to be frustrated and disappointed. They feel stress and distress. They lack a feeling of well-being.

A master of gratitude will use all occurrences to gain greater mastery over gratitude. Each time something doesn't work out the way he would like, he remembers to feel grateful for all the times that things do work out well. This pattern of thinking brings a person feelings of happiness and joy.

When a machine breaks down, one can be happy for all the times when machines do work. If someone doesn't remember to do what he said he would, a master of gratitude is grateful for all the times this person did remember. And he is grateful for other people remembering to do what they said they would. When stores run out of things, it's a reminder to be grateful for all the times this store and other stores had the things that are needed and wanted. A message not given is a reminder to be more careful to give over messages oneself, and to be grateful for all the messages that he did receive. A letter not received on time is a reminder to be grateful for all the letters that are received on time. All the many things that don't work out the way they usually do are reminders to be grateful for all multitude of things that do work out.

A person who integrates this pattern will live a life of gratitude and happiness.

Some people might be afraid that if they are grateful when things don't work out, they might be causing more things not to work out, but in truth it works the opposite way. If you thank a person who did not do what you were expecting him to do for all the times he did do what you expected him to do, you will still be even more grateful when he does what you were hoping he would do. And your positive response will be motivating. When you are grateful to our Creator for causing good things to happen in your life, you will not be doing anything to lessen the good things from happening.

What are ten things that recently worked out the way you wanted them to, for which you are grateful? Allow yourself to feel grateful for them now. The next ten times that something trivial and minor doesn't work out the way you would like, go down your mental list of what you are grateful for. This way you will be building up a pattern of letting the negative remind you of what has been positive in your life.

"I lost my job and felt terrible," a forty-year-old rabbi related. "I had devoted a lot of time and energy to teaching and helping the members of my congregation. Everyone agreed that I did a good job, but I was told that the more influential members of the congregation wanted someone who was more dynamic and outgoing than I was.

"At first I was devastated. I didn't know where to turn. Then I spoke to an older rabbi who had been through many life challenges. 'What would you advise me to do now?' I asked him.

"He said, 'Before you begin looking for a new position, you need to think the type of thoughts that will help you be resilient. If you go on interviews feeling as bad as you do now, you will either seem too pessimistic about the future or too resentful about the past. You need to let go of this distress that you are experiencing.

"'You were grateful for the job when you did have it, weren't you?'

"'Very much.'

"'Then keep that gratitude foremost on your mind. Instead of feeling bad about losing that job, feel grateful for all the many benefits you gained from the job. Be grateful now to the people who hired you. Be grateful to the people who helped raise the money for your salary. Be grateful for the opportunity to teach and to counsel. Be grateful for all the major benefits and all the minor benefits. This will immediately make you feel better. Moreover, when you go for interviews, if you are still able to maintain gratitude for the past, you will be in a much better state of mind and you are manifesting a character trait that will be an asset on any new job.'

"I found this advice invaluable," the rabbi concluded. "At first I found it difficult to implement. But I am now very grateful for it. It has been a key factor in living a much better life."

28.

Honoring Father and Mother

The foundation of the commandment to honor our father and mother is our obligation to be grateful to those who have done positive things for us. Being ungrateful is a negative trait and is repulsive to G-d and to people (*Sefer Hachinuch*, Commandment 33).

Every word we say to show our respect and thanks to our parents is an expression of our gratitude. So is every act we do that expresses respect and thanks.

Keep upgrading the level of your honor of your father and mother. We see from the Talmud that regardless of how much a person honored his parents, there is no amount that is sufficient. There is always more one can say and do. Keep learning from others about more possibilities. Notice the positive things that other people do for their parents and see how you can apply some of these things.

Think about ways that you might be deficient in honoring your parents. Resolve to correct those deficiencies.

From time to time explicitly tell your father and mother that you are grateful for all that they have done for you. Some people who aren't used to expressing their gratitude might feel a bit uncomfortable about doing this. "They know I'm grateful," they say as a way of avoiding doing what they find difficult. The more difficult it is to do something, the greater the action. So think of a time to tell your parents that you are grateful, and, at the first opportunity, follow through.

I met an eighty-year-old man who kept praising his father and telling me what a wonderful person he was.

"How long ago did your father pass away?" I asked him.

"Close to forty years," he replied.

"But you talk about your father as if he had recently died!"

"That's because he's constantly at the forefront of my mind. I am tremendously grateful for all that my father did for me. I can never thank him enough."

29.

A Tale of Two Guests

The Talmud (*Berachos* 58a) tells the story of two guests, one a good guest and the other a bad guest.

A good guest is one who, when invited to someone's home, sees everything with a good eye. When he is served food and drink, he thinks and says, "My host has put in so much effort on my behalf. Look at the meat he gave me to eat. Look at the wine he gave me to drink. Look at all the bread he served me. All that he did, he did for me."

A bad guest is one who, when invited to someone's home, sees everything with a bad eye. When he is served food and drink, he thinks and says, "My host didn't really have to work very hard for me. I ate only one slice of bread. I ate only one piece of meat. And I drank only one cup of wine. All the work and effort were really for his wife and children."

These two people might even be guests of the same host at the same time, but each one may have a totally opposite view of what happened. A bad guest belittles what he has gained from the other person. And even though he has to admit and acknowledge that he did gain something, he claims that the benefactor didn't truly do it for him; he did it for his own family. He might even claim, "He invited me as a guest. That's because he enjoys having company and likes to appear generous." He is utterly ungrateful.

The good guest builds up an appreciation for all that he received. He focuses not only on the meal as a whole, but on each part of the meal. He is grateful for each detail. Moreover, he appreciates all the time, work, effort, and even money that his host had to spend on him. He is full of gratitude.

These are two patterns of thinking that create very different realities. In what ways are you a "bad guest" and in what ways are you a "good guest"? Resolve to model the "good guest."

Think back to different people whose homes you have been invited to as a guest. Right now, upgrade the way you look at those visits. Right now, see everything your host did for you with the eyes of a good guest. Increase your gratitude for each and every detail of each and every host. This will be a great exercise in upgrading your attribute of gratitude.

When thinking about how the talmudic metaphor of the two guests applies to them, many people are surprised at how much they resemble the ungrateful guest. Here are some of comments that were made:

"I was married at a later age than usual and frequently ate at people's homes. Every once in a while it was difficult for me to find a place for Shabbos. After I was married and often had guests, I saw the efforts that my wife and I put into making our guests comfortable. As a guest myself, I hadn't realized how much went into having company. More time was spent cleaning up the house and making fancier meals. At times, either my wife or I wasn't up to having guests. Looking back, I saw how feelings of resentment at not being invited to people's homes, even though this was a rarity, were much stronger in my mind than the gratitude I had towards the people who had invited me over."

"I realized that when strangers invited me over to their homes, I was more grateful to them than I was to my parents, who had had me in their home from the time I was an infant. I took it for granted that since I was their child, of course I am at their home; it's really my home also. After hearing about the two types of guests, I wanted to be like the good guest, and I recalled the many details of how much my parents had done for me throughout my entire life. This increased the level of gratitude I expressed to my parents."

A husband said, "My wife has made countless meals for me. I have a lot to be grateful for in many ways. But I realize that when the meals are late or don't consist of the foods I like best or haven't been cooked well enough, my complaints are much longer and stronger than my thanks for when meals are on time and the food is the way I like. I have resolved to stop complaining about what I don't like, and to increase my expressions of gratitude for what I do. Not only does this make my wife happier, but I see that I have no need to complain. Motivating with sincere gratitude is more effective than complaining and hoping that this negativity will bring about positive changes."

30.

What Your Gratitude Can Do for Someone

*W*hen you express your gratitude to someone, not only do you give him good feelings in the present, you also motivate him to do more good in the future. You help upgrade the recipient's self-image and you show that the good he has done is appreciated.

Many people are not aware of the positive impact they have had on others. They need to hear it. When you tell someone that his words made a difference in your life, your words will make a difference in his life.

Someone who is working at a job might feel unappreciated. Expressing your gratitude for what he has done could make all the time and effort he puts into his job feel much more worthwhile.

Someone cooks meals for you. You might say, "Thank you," but the person can feel that you are just being polite. When you go out of your way to express your appreciation in such a manner that the cook sees you mean it sincerely, all the cooking in the future will be done with the positive feeling that the cooking is appreciated.

What has the gratitude of others done for you? The more aware you are of how much the gratitude of others has done for you, the more aware you will be of what your gratitude can do for others.

There will probably be some people who won't be able to think of an answer. Their first response might be, "Nobody is ever grateful to me."

If you feel this applies to you, then keep your eyes and ears open for someone's expression of gratitude. And the first time you notice someone's gratitude, you can tell him, "I am tremendously grateful for your gratitude. You can't imagine how much it means to me."

And you might not be able to imagine how much your gratitude can mean to him.

An elderly retired teacher lived in a nursing home. He had retired fifteen years before and rarely had visitors. He was lonely and often felt that the many years he had devoted to his students were long forgotten. He still read a lot, and his mind was active, but the thought that nobody remembered him saddened him. His wife had died seven years before and his three children, who lived far away, rarely visited. They did call him regularly, but day in, day out, the thought weighed on his mind that what he had done for so long was not appreciated.

Then one day he received a call from a former student who asked if it would be all right if he and some of his friends from school came to visit. The retired teacher was thrilled. "Of course, it's more than all right. I look forward to your visit."

Over twenty now grown-up students surprised him with a gala party in his honor. Each former student got up to speak and expressed appreciation for what the teacher had done for him. They related that much of their success in life was because of his positive influence on them. They taped the speeches and took many pictures.

For the rest of his life those pictures made him glow. He was remembered. The work he had done lived on. He had asked them to call him every once in a while, which they did. They also told their friends that their calls would be appreciated. Each call was a symbol of gratitude that added much light to his life.

31.

Who Helped You Accomplish What You Did?

*W*henever someone accomplishes anything, there are always other people who have been instrumental in helping that person to accomplish. Be grateful to the people who have helped you to accomplish throughout your life.

The Talmud relates that the great sage Rabbi Akiva told his many students that they owed a debt of gratitude to his wife for the Torah that he had taught them. Rabbi Akiva had begun as a simple shepherd. It was only because of his wife, Rachel, that he had devoted many years to study, and through this became a teacher to multitudes of students. While Rabbi Akiva was the one who had actually taught them, it was only because of the great sacrifice of his wife that he was able to become the great scholar that he did. (See *Sichos Mussar* of Rabbi Chaim Shmuelevitz, p. 318. Mentioning Rabbi Chaim Shmuelevitz, Rosh Hayeshiva of Mir in Jerusalem, gives me a feeling of obligation to express my gratitude for the many times I have heard him speak and the positive influence his talks have had on my life.)

Be grateful to the teachers who have taught you what you needed to know to be able to accomplish.

Be grateful to the schools that have helped you gain the knowledge that you now have that enabled you to accomplish. Those schools have enabled you to meet the teachers that have helped you.

Think about your major accomplishments in life. Who are the main people who have helped you to accomplish? Who are some of the people who had seemingly minor roles in your accomplishments, but without whom you might not have accomplished what you did? At times there will be people without whose help you could still have accomplished, but because of them you accomplished more than you would have without them. Be grateful to them for that.

I met someone who kept boasting that he is a self-made person. "I did it all on my own," he said. "No one helped me."

"Aren't there some people who have helped you to whom you can be grateful?" he was challenged.

"I'm the one who had the ideas and I'm the one who made certain that those ideas would be implemented," he said.

"Imagine that you would have been all alone on a desert island. Could you still have accomplished what you did?"

"Of course not," he said. "But still, I am what I am because of myself."

"You want to be honest about this, don't you?" he was asked.

"Of course," he replied.

"So if you were to make a list of which people were absolutely necessary for your accomplishments, which people would you include on your list?"

I saw from the look on his face that this way of looking at the entire situation was a bit different than his often-mentioned boast that he had done it all alone.

"Did some people do favors for you that helped you out? Did anyone lend you money or other resources that made it possible? Did anyone give you helpful suggestions? Did you hire people to do some of the tasks that you didn't have time to do yourself? Did anyone supply you with information that made it possible?"

A few days later he called me up and acknowledged, "I see that before I was almost blind as to how much other people have helped me. I have resolved to be more grateful from now on."

32.

Gratitude for Encouragement

*W*ho has encouraged you throughout your life?

Be grateful to each and every person who has said things to you that have given you the inner strength to do what you might not have done without that encouragement.

There are projects and courses of action that we might not have followed through on. We might have been ready to give up. We were feeling discouraged. We might have thought that we were wasting our time and effort. We might not have realized that we had the necessary skills, talents, and intelligence. Someone believed in our abilities. Someone was willing to tell us that we should continue going further. Be grateful for what those people have done for you.

Think now of people who have encouraged you at different stages of your life. What did they say to you? They might have told you that they saw inner strengths, skills, and talents you weren't fully aware that you had. Or perhaps you knew that you had them, but you didn't realize their extent. At times it wasn't the exact words themselves that made the difference. It was the inner feeling they had that they conveyed to you. Express your gratitude.

At first you might not have realized how much those words of encouragement would help you. Only much later did you look back and see how someone's encouragement at a crucial moment changed the course of your life.

Many words of encouragement aren't tremendously dramatic and life-transforming. But they gave you more energy. They made a heavy situation much lighter. They made you feel much better than you would have otherwise felt. Be grateful.

When you are more aware of how much you personally have gained from the encouragement of others, you are more likely to offer words of encouragement to others. And when you do, and you find that you have helped others because of the help that someone bestowed on you, you will be even more grateful to that person.

Someone told me that a phrase would run through his mind quite frequently. It was, "You can do it!" Whenever something he was doing seemed to become too difficult, he would hear an inner voice saying, "You can do it!" Whenever he felt too tired to take care of something that he knew he had to take care of, he heard this inner voice saying, "You can do it!" This seemed so much a part of him that he took it for granted and didn't give it much thought. When it was suggested to him that he think about gratitude for those who had encouraged him, he remembered a childhood incident. He had an older brother who had repeated this phrase to him a few times. His brother was just three years older, but when he was little, those three years made a big difference. Without his realizing it, those words stayed with him and helped him innumerable times.

Over the years he had grown apart from his older brother; there was a lot of tension in their relationship. They tended to avoid each other. After realizing how much his brother's encouragement had helped him, his sense of gratitude motivated him to renew their relationship. His positive feelings towards his brother aroused positive feelings in return. They both found it almost miraculous that they now became so close.

33.

Gratitude for Inspiration

Rabbi Shalom Eisen, a prominent authority of Torah law, came to Rabbi Isser Zalman Meltzer, the head of Eitz Chaim Yeshiva, and personally invited him to his son's bar mitzvah, which would be a long distance from Rabbi Meltzer's home. When Rabbi Meltzer heard about the bar mitzvah of his student's son, he said with great emotion, "It's already the bar mitzvah of your son. Time passes by so quickly. It's amazing how time flies." These thoughts were repeated a few times.

Rabbi Meltzer was elderly and it was difficult for him to walk great distances. Therefore, on the Shabbos of the bar mitzvah, which was a very hot day, Rabbi Eisen was very surprised to see Rabbi Meltzer coming in to wish him mazel tov, and he ran to greet his Rebbe.

"It is difficult for me to walk such a distance," Rabbi Meltzer said, "but I felt an obligation of gratitude to come. When you invited me to the bar mitzvah of your son, I started thinking about how fast time flies. I gained from these thoughts, and therefore I felt it proper to join in your celebration." (Cited in *Growth Through Torah*, from *B'derech Eitz Hachaim*, vol. 2, p. 418.)

We benefit tremendously from moments of inspiration. When we are inspired, we think more elevated thoughts than we usually do. We are motivated to upgrade our words and our actions. Be grateful to those who inspire you.

Some people might inspire you because they express lofty thoughts. As you think those thoughts, you feel higher spiritually than you ordinarily do.

And some people might inspire you in ways in which they themselves might not have been aware.

By expressing gratitude for those who inspire you, you are making a statement that you appreciate those moments of inspiration. You realize how precious and valuable they are. And this adds more inspiration to your moments of inspiration.

Think of some of the people who have inspired you. What can you say or do to express gratitude for that inspiration?

34.

List of Gratitude Statements

*H*ere is a list of gratitude statements that are worth reading a number of times in order to integrate them into your speech. Even though you might have been aware of them before you read the list, when you have recently read such a list, you are more likely to say these or similar statements.

When you read this list, you will benefit the most by reading it out loud and imagining that you are saying these words of gratitude to someone who has done something for you.

I always remember how you helped me when I needed it.

I am grateful for all the many things you have done for me.

I am grateful for your gratitude.

I appreciate what you did for me.

I thank you from the bottom of my heart.

I'll always remember your kindness.

I'll never forget what you did for me.

Knowing that someone cares so much is tremendously valuable.

No matter how many times I thank you, I can't thank you enough.

Thank you for doing so much for me.

Thank you for sharing your knowledge with me.

Thank you so very much for all the help.

Thank you! Thank you! Thank you!

Thanks a million.

That was deeply meaningful.

That was great.

That was very thoughtful of you.

That was wonderful.

The feedback you gave me made a world of a difference.

The time and effort you spent on doing this for me is greatly appreciated.

You can't imagine how good you made me feel.

You have been a great role model.

You have been a source of strength for me.

You have made all of this possible.

You made my day. Thank you.

You were heaven-sent.

Your assistance saved me.

Your consideration and concern meant a lot to me.

Your encouragement made a great difference.

Your feedback taught me a lot.

Your going out of your way for me is appreciated beyond words.

Your guidance had a major impact on me.

Your help was a lifesaver.

Your help was greatly appreciated.

Your input was very beneficial.

Your insights have changed my life.

Your kind words helped me more than you can imagine.

Your kindness means a lot to me.

Your moral support and practical advice have helped me immensely.

Your suggestions worked wonders.

Your tireless work is tremendously appreciated.

Your understanding gave me the inner strength that I needed to handle the challenge.

Your wisdom has enlightened me.

Your words have given me life.

What you did for me was terrific.

What you told me is more precious than gold.

When I think of kindness, I think of you.

Without your help I would not have made it.

Words can't express how grateful I am.

35.

Gifts that Express Gratitude

Giving gifts is a powerful way to express gratitude. When you give someone a gift, think about what this person would truly appreciate. What does this person need? What would this person like to have even if he doesn't actually feel a need for it now?

When you see an item that you feel would be perfect for giving someone as a gift, ask yourself, "To whom am I grateful who would appreciate this as a gift?"

Books are great gratitude gifts. A book can be read over and over again. And even when it is read only once, a book on the bookshelf is a frequent reminder that you are grateful.

There are many inexpensive items that would be greatly appreciated as a "thank you" gift.

If you want to make sure that what you will be buying someone as a gift is something that this person would truly appreciate receiving, think of someone you can consult. You might ask someone to ask the person for you, "Is there something that you probably would not buy for yourself but would appreciate someone buying for you as a gift?"

A general rule to keep in mind is, don't just get someone a gift that you personally would like to receive. Give what you think this individual would like.

I once met someone who is considered an expert gift-giver. "How did you develop your expertise?" I heard someone ask this person.

He answered, "I keep asking people, 'What are the gifts that you have appreciated the most?' I even ask this to strangers I meet in lines at stores. I have heard a tremendous amount of people answer this question. This has given me a strong sense of what different people appreciate as gifts."

36.

Acting "As If"

"*I* am a person who lacks feelings of gratitude. On a practical level, what can I do about it?" I was asked by a young man who sincerely wanted to become a better person.

This is a common question asked by people who find that reading and talking about a positive trait motivates them to want to improve, but isn't sufficient to make an actual change.

The classic answer to this question in reference to gratitude and other positive traits is to perform many acts of gratitude over time. Rambam tells us this in *Hilchos Dei'os*, chapter one. And the *Sefer Hachinuch* (mitzvah number 16) states that people are drawn after their actions.

This principle is expressed concisely in the formula: "Act as if!"

When you act as if you have already mastered gratitude, you are building up your level of gratitude right now. Even before you truly are a person of gratitude, by speaking and acting as if you were grateful, the intention of being grateful in thought and feeling leads you in the right direction.

When you find yourself in a situation that calls for gratitude, and you don't spontaneously know what to say or do, ask yourself, "If I were a grateful person, what would I say and do right now?"

Some people are hesitant about acting as if they were grateful. "It's important for me to be authentic. I highly value acting the way I really am," they obstinately claim.

This position can be challenged. "It's admirable to be authentic. And being authentically grateful is the goal. But right now your choice is between being authentically ungrateful or being a person who acts in a more elevated manner than he has as yet internalized. Speaking and acting as ungrateful as you really are will keep you where you are. If, however, you are willing to speak and act as if you were grateful, you will in fact be building up your character."

The winning argument is to ask oneself, "When you go out of your way to help someone, would you prefer he says or does nothing that would be an expression of gratitude, since this is his authentic self-centered way, or would you prefer he speaks and acts with the gratitude he wishes to eventually have?"

The answer is usually quite obvious.

I recently spoke to someone who feels that gratitude is a valuable attribute for him to develop further. Among other ideas, we spoke about the power of acting "as if." A few days later he called me up and said, "When you first mentioned the benefits of acting as if I were a master of gratitude, I didn't feel that this would be necessary for me. I consider myself a grateful person. But a short while later, someone called me up and related that he had met someone who had done many kind actions for people. This benefactor recently found out that one person whom he had helped out greatly had acted with gross ingratitude, and he was feeling hurt. A telephone call expressing my gratitude for what he had done for me would be highly meaningful at this time.

"My first reaction was that I should call this person as soon as possible to tell him that I am still grateful for his past kindnesses. But a number of things came up and I didn't make the call. Many hours later I remembered that I still needed to make that gratitude call. I was very tired and worn out and didn't feel like it. I was mentally grateful, but I wasn't in my gratitude state right then. However, I knew that if I wouldn't make the call right away, I might not get around to it later.

"What you told me about acting 'as if' came to mind. I said to myself, 'Let me put the power of acting "as if" into action, and I made the call. While I was dialing, it was out of a sense of acting as if I were more grateful right then. When the person I called expressed an intense appreciation for my gratitude call, I saw how good this made me feel. I then felt a true sense of gratitude for the past kindnesses this person had done for me."

37.

Tone of Voice of Gratitude

There are many different ways to say "thank you." We are not referring now to different verbal expressions of thanks, but rather to the tone of voice that is used to say "thank you."

There is a "thank you" that is said without any feeling or emotion. This can be a habitual, automatic reaction. It is said without any life or energy. It is said by rote. It's much better to say this kind of "thank you" than not to say it. But it's only the bottom level of what is possible.

There is a "thank you" that is said with the tone of voice of appreciation. You can tell from the way that it is said that the person who said it truly appreciates what was done for him. His heart is in what he is saying. This is a true expression of gratitude.

And then there is an enthusiastic, deeply felt "thank you." The tone of voice expresses a strong and intense feeling of gratitude. Some people reserve such a "thank you" for only super-special occasions. Only for something extraordinary would they express this kind of "thank you." Those who have elevated their level of gratitude, and truly feel a deep sense of gratitude for even smaller acts of kindness, will express their gratitude emphatically on a regular basis.

Imagine a home where everyone is grateful to everyone else for all the good that they do for them. There will be a lot of positive energy in that home.

Imagine a business or an organization where everyone feels grateful to everyone else for how they all gain from each other. There will be a lot of positive energy in that business or organization. People will enjoy working there and will enjoy visiting.

Be aware of how you sound when you are very grateful to someone. Remember this tone of voice so you can upgrade the way you express gratitude to others when you truly feel grateful, but are not then feeling as enthusiastic about it as this person deserves.

"Someone suggested that I should add more 'oomph' to the way that I express words of gratitude. But I argued, 'That's not me. I don't express myself with enthusiasm, and it won't sound natural if I try to.'

"The person who suggested this to me said that he understands why I am reluctant to try this out with people who already know me. They've gotten used to my usual lifeless way of talking, and will wonder if I'm all right if I suddenly start expressing gratitude with enthusiasm. So I was told to express gratitude with more energy to people who aren't familiar with my usual way of speaking. I can do this when I buy things in a store where people don't know me. I can do this when strangers give me directions how to get somewhere. I can do this when I buy stamps in the post office. I should remember the most enthusiastic 'thank you's' I've heard from others, and I can test it out as an experiment.

"To my great surprise I found that this was a lot of fun. Even though I felt self-conscious at first, those who didn't know me thought my fervent tone was my normal way of speaking. It was more enthusiastic than the way most people expressed thanks, but it didn't sound manic or strange to them.

"I added a little bit more enthusiasm to the way I thanked the people I knew. After they got used to this, I added a bit more enthusiasm. This added more positive energy to my entire life."

38.

There Is No Time Limit on Gratitude

There is no time limit on gratitude. If you realize in the present that you did not express gratitude to someone for something that he did for you a long time ago, don't think that it's too late to express gratitude. Whenever you remember past kindnesses and favors done, express your thoughts and feelings of gratitude.

The classic example of delayed gratitude is related in Megillas Esther, which is read in the synagogue on the holiday of Purim. King Achashveirosh had his written memoirs read to him, which recorded how Mordechai had saved the King's life. When the King was reminded of this, and was told that nothing special had been done for Mordechai as an expression of gratitude, the King gave an order to honor Mordechai. This was a crucial link in the chain of the hidden miracles that led to the saving of the entire Jewish nation.

We can learn from this the importance of writing down the kindnesses that someone else has done for you in order to express gratitude to that person later on.

At times someone might do something positive for you that at the time didn't seem like anything important. It appeared to be something minor and trivial. But as events unfold, you see that you gained immensely from that person's advice, suggestions, or help. When you realize the extent of the benefit you gained, your level of gratitude should be increased. Express this new level of gratitude.

You can express your feelings of gratitude to the same person for the same thing many times. Every time you tell someone that you are grateful to him, you make him feel good. There is no limit to the amount of times you can do this kindness.

I knew a person who greatly appreciated opportunities to do acts of kindness. He had a strong realization of how people appreciate being told that someone is grateful to them. At times he would go out of his way to ask someone for a minor favor. Then he would thank the person enthusiastically. And he would go over to that person a number of times to repeat how grateful he still felt for the kindness that this person did for him.

Some people would say to him, "But it was really nothing. It didn't take me much time or effort."

He would reply, "But I gained from what you did. I recall my grateful feelings and I want you to know that I still appreciate what you did for me."

39.

Accepting Gratitude

*W*hen someone expresses gratitude for something you have done, express your gratitude for that person's gratitude. By accepting that person's words of gratitude, you are making it more likely that this person will continue to express gratitude to others.

Look at the situation from the point of view of the people who tell you that they are grateful. What would they prefer that you would say? Most people would probably appreciate your being grateful for their gratitude.

Some people feel uncomfortable when others tell them that they are grateful. A common response of many people is, "It was nothing." In certain situations this might be the most appropriate thing to say. If you go out of your way to help someone and that person is the type who feels bad if he thinks he bothered someone or caused a lot of work, saying, "It was nothing," will be an act of kindness for that person. Now the person will feel better about your having gone out of your way for him.

When people express gratitude to you, let this remind you to become more grateful to others. Ask yourself, "What can I say to someone else to express my gratitude?"

A student shared with me, "I wasn't so careful to express gratitude to others. I would usually be polite and say, 'thank you,' but my heart wasn't in it."

"What awakened me to the value of expressing gratitude was that I went out of my way to help someone. It was very difficult for me to do what I did, but I did it anyway. The person thanked me, but I went away with a feeling that for all the effort I put into helping this person, he should have expressed gratitude with more emotion.

"A week later, I received a package from someone else with a gift that I appreciated. There was a card attached that said, 'Words alone can't express how grateful I am to you. Here is a token of my appreciation.' I saw how much I appreciated this gratitude. I wrote a note back to this person, saying that he can't imagine how much his gratitude meant to me. He then sent me a card saying that my gratitude for his gratitude meant a lot to him. From then on I had a much greater appreciation for what gratitude can mean. My expressions of gratitude have become much more expressive."

40.

Let People Know that They Should Feel Grateful to Others

*H*elp spread gratitude in the world. If you know that someone has done something that was beneficial to another person, let the recipient of the benefit know about it. Point out to him that he should be grateful to his benefactor.

In situations where the benefactor did not purposely want to keep the matter a secret, by telling the one who benefited from the kindness that he has something for which to be grateful, you are spreading positive feelings and good will among the Creator's children.

There are many instances where someone might know that another person did something for him, but he doesn't realize how difficult it was to do that kindness. It could have taken much longer than most people would have guessed. There could have been factors that would make something much more difficult than it would usually be. The person who benefited couldn't have realized these factors on his own. You might want to say, "Now that you realize how difficult it was for that person to do this for you, let him know that you appreciate his efforts and are grateful."

There are many people who have gained from others when they were much younger. When they were young children, various people did many things for them. Now, when they are old enough to fully appreciate what those people did for them, it could be pointed out to them that they should express their gratitude for what was done.

I once heard the following about a kind-hearted person who made it a very high priority to "love peace and pursue peace." If he ever heard someone speak negatively about someone else, he would go out of his way to see if he could find positive things that the person spoken against said or did for the person who spoke against him. When he found something positive to report, he would relate it in a way that was certain to have a positive effect. The gratitude felt by the person who heard about the positive things made it much more likely that in the future he would be more careful not to speak against that person again.

41.

Gratitude for Pointing Out Your Faults

At times, the best thing in the world that someone could do for us is to point out our faults and needless limitations. When we appreciate how we can develop ourselves once we realize what we were doing wrong, we will be grateful to the person who helps us grow and develop by pointing us in the direction that we need to go.

Imagine how you would feel if you were in a strange city and you were walking around in circles for a number of hours. Let's say you are the type of person who doesn't like to ask others for directions. Or you would gladly ask someone, but you don't speak the same language, or there is no one around to ask. And then someone comes over to you and asks, "What are you looking for?" When you tell him, he laughs and says, "I'm glad that you told me. You are way off. The place you need to go is on the other side of town. Here are the exact instructions you need to get there." You would be grateful to that person, wouldn't you?

We should be much more grateful to those who point out serious faults we have – faults that prevent us from being all that we could be spiritually, or faults that cause us problems when we interact with others, with a specific person or with people in general.

If someone were unwittingly doing something that would likely cause him a serious injury, he would be grateful to a person who pointed it out. This is the type of gratitude we should feel towards someone who points out our character defects that could destroy our lives, or at least cause us serious problems in life.

The natural tendency of most human beings is not to be joyful when people point out their faults and character defects. It takes courage to be open to listening to what others tell us about our need to improve ourselves. It takes great determination to become a better person in order to appreciate personal criticism. It takes a degree of honesty to acknowledge the validity of what a critical person tells us.

So when you feel gratitude towards someone who points out your faults, you can feel an inner sense of appreciation that you are able to appreciate the criticism. Your gratitude is an expression of your authentic desire to become a better and more elevated person. And you can be grateful to the person who criticized you for bringing out this awareness.

A student of mine told me the following:

I was complaining to a friend about how someone would frequently criticize me. "I can't take it," I whined. "It's so rough to be told over and over again that I have this or that fault."

"How do you feel when someone praises you?" the friend asked.

"I feel happy. It's enjoyable to hear someone praise me."

"Do you feel grateful?" the friend asked me.

"I certainly do. It makes me feel much better about myself," I replied.

"Imagine how much more grateful you can be towards someone who points out your faults. This person isn't creating those faults. You are. He is telling you that he notices these faults in order for you to become a better person. What's truly better? Being told you already have done well and have a good quality when you already know this, or being told that you have a fault, in order to correct it and actually make yourself a better person than you were before? Wouldn't it be a sign of greatness on your part to be able to sincerely express gratitude?"

I had to admit that my friend was right. I had never looked at it this way before. Now I resolved to think back to people who had criticized me in the past. I was going to upgrade my feelings of resentment towards these people to feelings of gratitude. As I did this, I noticed that I was in fact speaking and acting better in the areas that had been pointed out to me as needing improvement.

42.

Mentally Prepare Your Mind for Gratitude

*S*ome people automatically prepare their mind for disappointment, resentment, and anger. They want to ask someone for a favor or make a request that could be mutually beneficial, but before they actually speak to the person, they imagine how disappointed and bad they will feel if that person refuses their request. They think about how resentful and angry they will become. This pattern of thinking is a mental preparation for negativity. When someone thinks this way in advance, his negative thoughts have an immediate and strong impact on his actual biochemistry and physiology. It will affect his facial expression, body language, tone of voice, and choice of words. The negativity he builds up in his mind makes it more likely that his request will be met with a refusal.

Mentally prepare yourself for gratitude. Think about how grateful you will be if the other person will agree to grant you what you want. Think about the positive feelings you will feel towards him. Think about how you will enthusiastically express your gratitude to him. As these thoughts go through your mind, your inner mind makes mental pictures of this happening. Your positive thoughts have an immediate and strong impact on your actual biochemistry and physiology. Your mental pictures of gratitude will affect your facial expression, body language, tone of voice, and choice of words. Your own positive feelings are likely to have a practical positive effect on the person with whom you are speaking. The positivity you build up in your mind makes it more likely that your request will be met with an agreement.

So before making a request, you always have a choice of two patterns. Thinking about the benefits of choosing to be grateful in advance makes this the most rational and sensible choice, doesn't it?

I spoke to someone who was very resistant to the idea of thinking of being grateful in advance.

"If I imagine how good I will feel if someone meets my requests and how grateful I will be, I am afraid that this will add greatly to the distress of my feeling disappointed if the person ends up refusing to help me out."

"But would you prefer to make it more likely that he will agree to help you or that he won't agree to help you?"

"Certainly, I want to make it more likely that he will help me. But I don't want to add to potential suffering by increasing my level of disappointment."

"A basic Torah concept is that when the Almighty wants you to have something, you will get it. If you aren't able to get something that you want, that means that ultimately the Almighty knows that it's better for you not to get what you think you should.

"Imagine that you ask someone for a thousand dollars, and he refuses. How would you feel?"

"I'd feel disappointed."

"But if after he refused to give you the thousand dollars, he immediately sat down and wrote you a valid check for ten thousand dollars, how would you feel then?"

"I'd be grateful he refused my first request, because he is giving me even more than I was hoping for."

"This is the Torah attitude of trust in the Almighty. Instead of suffering from disappointment, you will know that a seemingly negative aspect of a refusal will be the seed of something more positive for you in the long run. At times you will see this soon afterwards with total clarity. And at times it will take much longer to see this. But you can always know that this is how things will end up.

"With this in mind, isn't it worth starting out with a mental picture of the gratitude you will feel when the request is granted? Any disappointment you might feel if the request isn't granted will melt away when you realize that this refusal ultimately will be beneficial for you."

43.

Be Grateful for Past Benefits from Schools and Jobs

*W*hen a person leaves a school or a job for another school or job, he should keep in mind what he is grateful for. Even if he feels he is benefiting more from his new school or new job, he should remember what he gained in the past from the previous places.

The Talmud (*Bava Kamma* 92b) states, "Don't throw rocks into a well from which you have drunk water." There are opinions (see Shita Mekubetzes, ibid) that even though this is basically meant as a metaphor, the literal meaning should also be followed. Why? Because this teaches us that, out of gratitude, we should respect everything in this world that benefits us, and all the more so people who have helped us.

There are many reasons why a person might have been dissatisfied at a previous place. Nevertheless, he still gained and benefited from the people of that place. It's easy for someone to remember the negative aspects of previous places, especially if he left on less than friendly terms. He might want to throw verbal stones at the prior school or job. Our debt of gratitude tells us not only that we should not speak against that place, but that we should say or do things that are an expression of gratitude.

Look at the former place with a good eye. When you speak about it, begin your sentences with, "I am grateful to them for ..." When you do so, you are expressing your own positive character.

I met a person who was complaining about the previous company for which he had worked. He made it sound as if he had been there for a short time and hadn't gained very much from being there.

"How long did you work there?" I asked him.

"Close to fifteen years," he replied.

"Did you learn anything from being on that job?"

"Yes, that even if you work hard for someone, they still might fire you."

"O.K., that's one lesson in reality. But did you gain any skills and talents? Did being on that job help you feed your family?"

"Well, I do consider myself an expert now in a few areas because I worked at that company. And they did pay me a fair salary when I was there."

"Why did they fire you?"

"They told me that their business isn't doing as well as it used to and they couldn't afford to pay me as much as I deserve. But I'm still resentful towards them."

"How does it make you feel to just remember your complaints?"

"Not very good. I was there fifteen years. And everything that is associated with working there now makes me feel bad."

"And how would it make you feel if you were grateful for the benefits that you gained over all the years?"

"I would feel good. But I can't deny the reality that it wasn't fair that they let me go."

"Since gratitude feels so much better than resentment, and you don't lose anything by focusing on what you are grateful for, doesn't it make sense to fill your mind with gratitude? Right now it's not a question of whether or not you will have that past job. You don't have it. It's just a question of whether you will choose gratitude, which will make you feel good. You are causing yourself a lot of needless distress by overlooking what you can be grateful for."

"Put this way, it makes sense. I'm feeling better already."

44.

Gratitude for Those Who Protect You

*W*hen we see that an individual has done something to protect us, we easily feel grateful. For example, if we see a specific soldier, policeman, security guard, or fireman risking his life to save ours, we will automatically feel highly grateful. The challenge is to feel grateful to the soldiers, policemen, security guards, and firemen whose presence protects us even though we do not see an immediate threat.

Some people dismiss thoughts of gratitude by arguing, "They aren't doing this especially for me. And if this specific person wouldn't be there to protect me, someone else would." In fact, you are gaining greatly because this person is ready to risk death and injury. Be grateful.

When a soldier, policeman, security guard, or fireman sees that you are grateful to him, it makes his task a little bit easier. Expressing your gratitude shows him that you realize that what he is doing is meaningful to you. Your positive words are an act of kindness. But what he is doing for you is an even greater act of kindness. Be grateful.

There are many security checks that we must go through to prevent terrorists from harming us. Some people view those in charge of making those security checks as being nuisances.

May we merit world peace one day soon. But until then, there are people who protect us. As they are protecting us, they also enable us to increase our level of gratitude.

A person who spent a lot of time and effort to express gratitude to soldiers was challenged, "But ultimately it is G-d Who protects us. Why are you so grateful to these individuals?"

"If someone goes out of his way to help you financially when you need it, are you grateful?" he asked that person.

"Of course I am," was the reply.

"But isn't G-d the ultimate source of the money you get?" he asked.

"Yes. But I still have an obligation to be grateful to the people who are kind to me."

"The same applies to the soldiers whose willingness to risk their lives enables you to feel more secure. Moreover, those who express gratitude to soldiers actually increase their gratitude to G-d for His protection. Those who aren't grateful to the human beings they see are more likely to take the Almighty's protection for granted. Instead of decreasing gratitude to Hashem, expressing gratitude to soldiers increases feelings of gratitude to the Creator of us all."

45.

Contribute to the Welfare of a Place You Visit

There is a concept in the Torah that teaches that whenever we visit a place, we should do something for the welfare of that place out of gratitude.

The Torah (*Bereishis* 33:18) relates: "And Yaakov came in peace to the city of Shechem, which is in the land of Canaan, when he came from Padan-Aram, and he encamped before the city."

The Talmud (*Shabbos* 33b) states that when Yaakov encamped by Shechem, he instituted something for the welfare of the city. Rav said that he minted coins. Shmuel said that he established markets. Rabbi Yochanan said that he set up bathhouses for the residents of the area. The Midrash (*Bereishis Rabbah* 79:6) adds that whenever we benefit from a place, we must show our gratitude by doing something for its welfare.

What Yaakov did was significant. We won't always be able to do things to such a degree. But when we think about it, there will often be something we can do. Even if what we do is relatively minor, we are still expressing our gratitude.

Some people think: "I'm new in this place," or, "I'm not going to be here for very long." This mindset prevents us from giving the matter thought. And if we won't think about what we could possibly do for the benefit and welfare of a place, we are unlikely to come up with ideas.

Develop the habit of asking yourself, "What can I possibly do that would be of benefit to others?" When you ask questions, your mind focuses on finding answers. It's amazing how our minds do this.

Every individual has unique knowledge. We have all undergone many different experiences in our lives. We have been to different places. We have heard and read various ideas. Therefore it is highly likely that we can think of ideas that others won't necessarily consider.

The way to build up your personal data base of things you can do to benefit places is to ask yourself when you visit a different city, neighborhood, institution, or organization, "What positive things do I see that I'm not used to?" This way, you will notice things that you might not have noticed otherwise. Then you can share some of this knowledge when you visit other places.

I related this idea to someone who said to me, "I tend not to notice things. I don't consider myself creative. And I don't think that I will be able to find things to benefit places."

"You might not be able to think of things on your own," I acknowledged. "But here is an easy tool that will help you gain more knowledge about what to suggest. When you meet someone who is new to your area, ask him, 'Can you think of some positive things that they do or have in your city, neighborhood, institution, or organization that you don't see here?' Not everyone will have things to suggest. But some will. And then you will be aware of similar things that you can suggest to others in various place where you will be."

46.

Watch Your Words — They Create Your Life

The words you speak program and condition your mind. When you speak words of gratitude, you are programming and conditioning your brain and mind to experience more and more gratitude.

Speaking words of negativity and ingratitude program and condition your brain and mind to experience less and less gratitude and more and more misery.

Even if you don't spontaneously feel like verbally expressing gratitude, you would still be wise to speak this way. Your words create you. Each time you express gratitude, your words change you into a grateful human being.

You create your habits and your habits create you. By speaking words of gratitude regularly, you develop the habit of speaking words of gratitude. The more you keep up this habit, the easier it becomes to say even more words of gratitude. As you continue to speak words of gratitude, thoughts of gratitude are integrated into your mind and you will spontaneously think and speak this way.

Catch yourself whenever your words express a lack of gratitude. Instead of being upset with yourself for still lacking as much gratitude as you would like to have, be grateful that you are becoming more aware of your lapses. This awareness will enable you to be more careful from now on.

It would be a good idea to resolve that whenever you hear yourself saying something that is ungrateful, you immediately make five statements of gratitude.

"It hurt me when someone told me that I tended to be ungrateful. I looked at myself as a grateful person," a refined gentleman told me. "My parents told me frequently that it's important to be grateful, and I have numerous memories of feeling and expressing gratitude.

"I told myself that I need to be objective about this. To my great surprise, I found that I did tend to express much more ingratitude than I had thought I did. It was true that I was always polite and thanked people many times. But because I had perfectionistic standards, there was much that I was displeased with. My displeasure often stood out more than my gratitude for the positive aspects. I needlessly said far too many things that were expressions of a lack of gratitude.

"I made a commitment to express much more gratitude than I had been doing already. Even though I thought it was important to express my displeasure over what I found to be negative, I was going to make certain to have a higher ratio of sentences of gratitude to those of ingratitude. This resolution had a very positive effect on my general state of mind. I appreciated hearing, from a few people, that I have been more pleasant to be around lately."

47.

Focus on What You Do Want and How Grateful You Will Feel

*I*t is wise to focus on what you do want. It is easy to focus on what you don't want. Choose wisdom over ease.

When you focus on what you do want, your brain is focused on finding ways to get it. You think about how good you will feel when you get what you want. You think about how grateful you will be when what you want becomes a reality. This upgrades your level of gratitude in advance, and you gain good feelings now, in the present, because of what you anticipate for the future. A wise person is one who sees the outcome (*Tamid* 32). The outcome of thinking and speaking in terms of outcomes is that you will find it easier to create a better life.

For example, let's say a person has not reached the basic goals he wants to reach. He has a lot of negative traits that he would like to overcome. He frequently expresses unhappy and distressful emotional states. He has a low self-image.

There are two ways he can think about this. The easy way is to think: "It's awful that I haven't reached even the basic goals that I want to reach. It's terrible that I have so many negative traits. I really must change. Feeling unhappy and distressed much of the time is not what I want for myself. Having such a low self-image is a disaster in my life."

How does this make one feel? Awful. How conducive is this for gratitude? Not one bit.

Now imagine this same person in the same life situation with one essential difference. He has read the title of this section, "Focus on what you do want, and how grateful you will feel." He says to himself, "This makes sense."

He makes a strong commitment to think in outcome patterns. This would mean saying to himself, "I am going to focus on reaching my major life goals. I will keep thinking about what I actually need to do to succeed. I will read what I need to know. I will learn from knowledgeable people. I will keep going and following through until I reach my goals. I will feel wonderful and grateful when I succeed in reaching the goals. And keeping my mind on this eventual gratitude and joy gives me good feelings and positive energy to take action now."

When it comes to character traits, the outcome-thinking person will say to himself, "I will upgrade my character traits in all important areas. I will work on this for as long as it takes. I will enjoy every bit of improvement. I feel grateful that I am moving in the right direction. Even before I upgrade the way I speak and the way I act, just thinking in this direction is giving me a greater chance to succeed. I feel grateful about this positive approach."

When it comes to positive emotional states, the outcome-thinking person thinks to himself, "I resolve to gain mastery over the most positive emotional states. I will become a happy, joyful, courageous, patient, serene, grateful person. I will keep developing this until I become a master at these states and will teach others. I am grateful that I am thinking this way now, and I will make this my natural state of mind."

When it comes to self-image, the outcome-thinking person thinks to himself, "I resolve to develop a great self-image in a modest way. I will see myself positively, since I am the one who chooses my self-image. I am grateful that I am making this choice now and will keep choosing this way of thinking."

Does this mean that all one has to do is choose a positive direction and then everything will automatically be perfect? Of course not! But if you keep focusing on what you don't want, that is what your inner world will include. You will be creating much distress and won't be as likely to take positive action to create what you can. So be wise. Choose to think about the thoughts, words, and actions you do want. And be grateful that you were given the gift of a mind that can think in these life-enhancing ways.

I spoke to a professional counselor and asked him what he considered the main problems of life that people have and what approaches he suggests to solve them.

He said, "The main problem in many people's lives is that they mentally go in the wrong direction. There are stress-related issues, accomplishment-related issues, issues relating to emotions, relationships, and communication, and similar matters. But a key to why the problems sometimes last much longer than necessary is that some people keep their main focus on their distress and what is wrong. As soon as someone focuses on what can be thought, said, or done to improve a situation, solutions can be designed and created. If one solution isn't working, then alternatives can be found. But if someone keeps dwelling on the problem, that prevents him from finding a solution. So the problem lingers on. Once I can influence someone to keep his focus on what can be done to improve a situation, even situations that can't be completely solved can be dealt with in a way that will make life more enjoyable and less distressing."

48.

How Do I Teach My Children to Be Grateful?

*P*arents commonly ask, "How do I teach my children to be grateful?"

Be role models of gratitude yourself.

Let your children frequently hear that you are grateful to Hashem for all the good He has given you in your life.

Let your children frequently hear you say that you are grateful to your parents for what they have done for you and what they have taught you.

Let your children frequently hear that you are grateful for friends, relatives, and neighbors who have done things for you, recently and a long time ago.

Let your children frequently hear that you are grateful to them for the positive things they do.

Parents need to explicitly teach their children that gratitude is a very special character trait that we all need to develop and upgrade. Children need to be told to express a "thank you" when others do things for them. But all the lectures in the world aren't as powerful as your own gratitude serving as a role model for them.

When someone does something for your children, besides just telling them to be polite and say "thank you," you can tell them, "Gratitude is an important *midah* (character trait). Every time you thank someone, you are developing more and more gratitude. You can be happy each time you tell someone that you are grateful."

One way to help children learn gratitude is to add "tag questions" when you make gratitude statements. For example, "That was really nice of that person to offer to help us carry that heavy package, wasn't it?" "Their kindness to us deserves a big 'thank you,' doesn't it?"

A person who was criticized for lacking gratitude tried to defend himself by saying, "I lack gratitude because my parents never taught me to be grateful."

"How old are you now?" he was asked.

"Over forty," he replied.

"Right now I am going to teach you to be grateful. Whenever someone does something to help you in any way, feel grateful to that person for what he has done for you. And then tell that person, 'I am grateful to you for what you have done for me.' From now on, you can't claim that you weren't taught to be grateful. You were taught at this moment, for the rest of your life. I doubt if you honestly didn't know this already from the time you were quite young. It's just that you kept repeating this ridiculous statement that you weren't taught gratitude. You probably believed it since you repeated it so often. But after our discussion, if you ever catch yourself about to say you weren't taught gratitude, remember that you were taught it. And follow through."

"Of course I know that you are really right," he replied. "I guess I have to be a bit more mature and take responsibility for my patterns myself. I am grateful to you for pointing this out."

"See, you've already put your gratitude into practice."

49.

Keep Your Main Focus on What Your Children Do Right

*P*arents want their children to have positive qualities and not to have negative ones. By keeping your main focus on the qualities that you do want your children to develop, they will be developing the traits you want them to have. This automatically overcomes potentially negative traits.

When it comes to helping children develop gratitude, it's important to keep reinforcing their self-image of being grateful.

The natural state of young children is not to be grateful unless they are taught gratitude. It's normal for parents to see young children manifesting a lack of gratitude. Be careful not to mistakenly reinforce a self-concept of being ungrateful.

Spend much more time pointing out when children are grateful than when they are ungrateful. When a child does express gratitude to a parent, teacher, or other adults, one can say, "I respect how you are developing the trait of being grateful. Your attitude will help you live a joyful life."

If you see your child being ungrateful, phrase what you say in the pattern that King Solomon (*Mishlei* 12:8) calls, "The words of the wise heal." That is, point out to them what they need to say and do to be grateful.

For example, with even a blatant example of a lack of gratitude, you can say, "This is a wonderful opportunity to now become more grateful. Think of how much you benefited from what this other person did for you, and tell him that you are grateful."

Be patient. With some children it might take a long time until they integrate gratitude. And you personally will be upgrading your own attribute of patience.

Someone who had to struggle long and hard with his self-image shared with me that his parents wanted him to become more grateful. Unfortunately, they did this in a counterproductive manner.

They would frequently tell him, "You are so ungrateful for all that we do for you."

They kept a constant vigil trying to catch him being ungrateful.

"If you weren't so ungrateful, you wouldn't be giving us such a rough time," they often said.

"If you weren't so ungrateful, you would go to sleep on time."

"If you weren't ungrateful, you would do your homework without us having to keep telling you to do it."

"I can't believe how ungrateful you are."

"Being so ungrateful will give you a miserable life."

If these parents had made it their goal to prevent this son from having gratitude towards them, they couldn't have been more successful at it.

In adulthood this fellow realized that even though his parents had used the wrong approach, their intentions were for his benefit. He eventually learned to forgive them and, little by little, worked on developing gratitude for the many good things they had done for him.

50.

Not Using Gifts Until Thanking

*I*n *A Daily Dose of Kindness* by Rabbi Shmuel Greenbaum, an anonymous mother wrote that after her son's bar mitzvah, she told him he could not use or enjoy any of his gifts until he first wrote a thank-you note. She related, "Everyone told me later that it was so nice to receive a thank-you note from my son, in his handwriting, and so soon after the occasion. Most people got their thank-you notes within the first week."

She added, "I learned this rule from someone else, and it was great advice, not to use a gift until you have thanked the donor for it. I was a very proud mother when people told me how well-mannered my son was."

One doesn't need to wait until a bar mitzvah to teach the lesson of gratitude to one's children. Gifts and presents at any age can be the source material for a practical lesson in making gratitude an integral part of oneself. Any gift received can serve as a powerful lesson in becoming more grateful.

Parents should use positive wording to get this point across. "This is such a nice gift. You will be able to use it as soon as you write a thank-you note or make a 'thank-you' telephone call." This is much better than saying, "You can't use this until you write a thank-you note or make a 'thank-you' telephone call." With the positively worded presentation, the "thank you" is what enables the child to use the gift. With the negatively worded presentation, the "thank you" is what prevents the child from using the gift until it is taken care of. Let gratitude be associated with good feelings, not the opposite.

I shared the above idea with someone, who later wrote to tell me that he thought of writing a gratitude letter to Hashem each morning for a week. This is the first gratitude letter he wrote:

Dear Hashem,

Right now I am typing this gratitude letter to You on my computer. I thank You for the computer to write this on. And I thank You for the energy to move my fingers to be able to type this. And I thank You for the eyes to see what I am writing. And I thank You for the chair that I am sitting on and the desk that holds the computer.

I thank you for Your oxygen that You are giving me to be able to breath to keep alive. And I am grateful to You for my being alive. I really should have mentioned this first, but I am writing this to You in the order of my thinking of these ideas.

I thank You for my memory that enables me to remember how to spell. This can be taken for granted, but not when one knows how fragile memory can be.

I thank You for my being able to hear the sounds that I now hear. And I thank You for enabling me to hear all the words of Torah that I have already heard. I thank You for enabling me to hear the songs and music that have enriched my life.

I thank You for my family and I thank you for my friends. I thank you for the electricity that enables me to be cool when it is hot outside. I thank you for the electricity so I can drink cold water and I thank you for the water.

I thank You for giving me so much for which to be grateful.

I pray to You to help me remember to write you a thank you letter each morning. This way I will be thanking you before I continue benefiting from Your kindnesses throughout the day.

Thank you,

Your grateful child and servant

51.

Judging Favorably

*I*f someone isn't as grateful to you as you think he should be, you have a choice. One choice is to judge the person negatively. With this choice, one assumes that the person who isn't grateful has negative character traits and lacks gratitude. The one who makes this choice is likely to feel resentful. Even if he isn't resentful, he is likely to feel negative feelings about the person he has judged negatively.

The other choice is to judge the person on the side of merit. Judge him favorably. We never know all the facts of a situation. We are always missing part of the entire picture. Repeat this last sentence at least ten times: "We are always missing part of the entire picture."

Maybe the person is much more grateful than you think. Maybe, for some reason, it is difficult for him to verbalize the grateful feelings that he does feel. Maybe he had a number of experiences in which people reacted to his expressions of gratitude in a way that made him feel bad. Perhaps, as a result, he has drastically toned down the way he thanks people.

Maybe he sent you a thank-you note, but it got misplaced. Maybe he called you a few times and left a message on your answering machine, but somehow it got erased. Maybe he would like to thank you, but kept pushing it off until he could do a more perfect job of expressing his gratitude. He meant to contact you, but as time passed, it slipped his mind. Since he thought of thanking you, when he thinks about thanking you he sort of remembers that he already thanked you. Maybe you were distracted when he said thank you. You didn't hear him, but he did thank you.

Maybe someone told you that he isn't grateful for some significant things that you did for him, but he truly is. Perhaps the person who told you the incorrect report heard it in a way that greatly distorted the facts. Many reports are false.

When you judge someone favorably, you fulfill a Torah commandment, even if the reality is not what you assumed it to be.

When you have a choice of judging someone favorably or negatively, if you judge the person negatively and are wrong, your negative assumption is unfairly painting a negative picture about this person, and you are missing out on fulfilling the good deed of judging this person favorably.

On the other hand, if you wrongly judged someone favorably and assumed that he was more grateful than he was, you don't lose anything. Moreover, you will feel more positively about this person, and he in turn is likely to feel more positively about you, so you both gain.

The Sages say, "Don't judge another person until you reach his place." You can't know everything that is going on in his life. Perhaps he is experiencing many difficulties, life challenges, or suffering. His mind wasn't clear enough to have the gratitude that he should. It could be his needs are so great that what you did was just a drop in an ocean. You view what you did as major, but to him it was only minor. He needs your compassion, not your resentment.

Creatively try to think of different ways to judge this person favorably. Knowing some experts at judging people favorably, I can testify that those who master this attribute live more joyful lives and interact more harmoniously with others.

Reuven shared with me the following story: "I went out of my way to help someone a number of times. I felt that I was motivated from a sincere desire to help this person, and I didn't feel that I helped him out with ulterior motives. But I felt bad when he gave me a cold 'thank you' and didn't speak in a friendly manner to me. I wondered why he wasn't more grateful. I didn't think I should say anything to him about it, because I felt that if I did, he would feel very uncomfortable. But the thought gnawed at me, 'Why wasn't he more grateful?'

"Eventually I did raise the issue with him. 'I'm curious. I'm not asking you to be more grateful than you actually are. But I thought that you might be friendlier towards me. Is there anything that I said or did that causes you to be so distant?'

"I'm glad that I brought the issue up with him. He told me that someone had told him that I had spoken against him. And even though he was grateful towards me for what I had done for him, he felt cold towards me because he thought that I had put him down. Someone completely misunderstood what I had actually said. I explained what I had said and he accepted my explanation. From then on, we have been on very friendly terms."

52.

Ask for Gratitude

Wanting people to be grateful for what we did for them is a strong human desire. The highest level to strive for is to be able to transcend the need for gratitude. Our love of doing kindness for others should be so strong and pleasurable that whether or not someone is grateful shouldn't take away the good feelings we have when we say or do things for others. But until someone reaches this high level, it is natural to want other people to be grateful.

If you want someone to be more grateful to you than he is, or if he seems to utterly lack gratitude, it is easy to say the wrong thing. Look at these counterproductive patterns:

"Why are you so ungrateful?"

"How come you aren't as grateful as you should be?"

"It hurts me greatly that you aren't grateful to me. I resent it!"

"I am furious that I work so hard for you and you are ungrateful!"

These and similar statements are likely to make the other person defensive, and often put him into a counterattack mode: "You aren't grateful to me, either!"

The solution to wanting more gratitude and not yet getting it is to ask for it directly. Ask for gratitude in a tone of voice that will make it easier for the other person to accept your request.

"Your gratitude would be very meaningful to me."

"I appreciate it greatly when you express your gratitude."

"I realize that maybe I shouldn't need gratitude, but so far I do, and your expressing gratitude to me is like sunlight for a flower."

"When you express gratitude to me, it makes me so happy that you will gain a lot by doing so."

You can modify these sentences to patterns that make you feel comfortable. But the pattern you use should be worded positively and expressed in a pleasant tone of voice.

The challenge of asking for gratitude is that it is easy to think, "I shouldn't need to ask for gratitude. This person should express it on his own."

Yes, he should. But we always have to deal with reality, not the way we would like things to be. So if you want gratitude and you're not getting it, it's wise to ask for it in a way that has a better probability of getting the reaction you want. You both gain.

A sixty-year-old grandmother was bitter and resentful. "Nobody is grateful to me for all the work I do for them. My employers where I have been working for over twenty years only point out what they don't like. They never express gratitude. My husband only rarely says anything that sounds like gratitude. My children keep asking me to do things for them and seem ungrateful for all the many things I have done for them throughout the years. My grandchildren aren't grateful for the gifts I give them. They do say a polite 'thank you.' But that's far from the gratitude I would like to receive. My neighbors don't express enough gratitude for the favors I do. And I could go on and on for a long time."

The rebbitzen she spoke to said, "Changing the character traits of even one other person is difficult. And changing the traits of many people is even harder. But I can give you a tool that is likely to improve the situation."

"What is it?"

"Ask people for gratitude."

"But I can't do that. People should know on their own that they should be grateful. I would feel embarrassed to ask explicitly for gratitude."

"Most people feel the way you do," the rebbitzen said. "It's often easier to just stay resentful and bitter than to ask for what you want. But it's so much wiser to ask. If the other person doesn't give you what you want, you don't lose anything. You are at the same place you were before you asked. And you can feel good knowing that you tried. When you ask in ways that are mutually respectful, in a calm tone of voice, many people will be happy to meet your request. Even if they aren't totally happy about it, your request is reasonable and valid, and they are likely to realize that they haven't been as grateful as they should have been."

"But I will feel foolish if they make fun of my request."

"Gratitude is an obligation. And it's wrong to make fun of another person," said the rebbitzen. "If someone else doesn't meet his obligation and does something wrong, he is the one who is acting foolish. What you are asking for is a normal thing to want."

Even before trying out the advice, the grandmother felt relief. She realized that while this seemed quite obvious, she never before felt that she had a right to ask for gratitude. Being given permission to do so would make it easier for her, and she knew that this solution would be helpful regardless of the outcome.

53.

Go from Worry to Gratitude

$\mathcal{W}$orry is the emotional distress that one causes oneself by thinking about something distressful that might happen at some future moment. The thoughts you think in the present create your present feelings. When the thoughts on your mind are pleasant or joyful thoughts, your entire inner system reacts accordingly. Your breathing rate changes, your brain waves change, your blood pressure changes, your energy level changes, your hormones change, your heartbeat changes, your immune system changes, your muscle tension changes, your facial expression changes, your posture changes, and your tone of voice changes. All these areas change counterproductively when you needlessly cause yourself anxiety by thinking worrisome thoughts. These changes happen instantly.

The future one worries about could happen in a long time from now or in a very short time from now. But worry is always about imagining, in pictures or words, a situation that you think will be distressful, and, instead of waiting until the future to feel bad, feeling bad right now. Since worry comes from thoughts, when you think more positive thoughts, you will feel better.

Worry always holds a seed of gratitude. Since you are worried that something will be distressful later, that means that at this moment in time you are really in a better situation than you think you will be in later. So you can be grateful that right now you are better off than you think you might be later on.

How many times in the past have you worried about things that might be problematic later, but those things you worried about never happened? Anyone who worries has certainly experienced this many times. You can be tremendously grateful about all those things, individually and together, right now. You can say to yourself, "I am so grateful that many of the things that I've worried about never happened."

How many times in the past have you worried about things potentially going wrong that later did go wrong, but the situation was much easier to deal with than you had imagined? I'm certain this has happened many times. You can be grateful now that things were better than you had thought they would be. You can also be grateful that you had the inner strength to handle challenges, difficulties, and even adversity positively or in ways contributing to growth.

Right now, think about how you have gained from all the things that you've worried about. Think of character traits that you have already strengthened and developed. Think of more character traits that you can develop now from those memories. Be grateful for all of this. Even if you haven't yet developed those positive traits, knowing that you can, and thinking about this now, gives you something for which to be grateful.

Now, in your inner mind, tell yourself, "Every time I begin to worry, I will immediately think of something for which to be grateful." Repeat this enough times until you feel that your inner mind will automatically go into gratitude mode as soon as it's aware that it's in worry mode.

Go from worrisome thinking to solution-oriented thinking. Ask yourself, "What possible solutions can I think of now?" Some people do this by writing down ten possible outrageous solutions. These solutions might be based on things happening that don't seem realistic. It seems most likely that they won't happen. But this brainstorming increases your creativity, and your inner mind can go from the unrealistic to the very practical. And then be grateful that this process makes you feel better. And when you do find a solution that works, be very grateful for that. And right now, be grateful for all the solutions that worked for other things in the past.

A person who used to worry a lot told me, "I used to be a major worrier. I would worry from the moment I woke up in the morning until I went to sleep at night. I always found many things to worry about. Even when things were going well, I worried that they wouldn't continue that way. It took me many years of working on my thoughts and feelings to overcome my tendency to worry. When I am tired out and exhausted, sometimes I still worry. But after proper rest, my mind thinks more objectively and clearly. I then think in positive, constructive ways.

"By overcoming worry myself, I know firsthand how much distress and pain worry causes. One of my goals in life is to help other people overcome worry and to live a happier life. I have helped many people. They know that I can relate to what they are feeling when I describe my own suffering from worrying about things that didn't happen, or weren't as bad as I had imagined.

"Looking back at my life, I am now very grateful for having experienced so much worry myself. This has given me the motivation and ability to help many people. This has given me many opportunities for kindness. My mission has given my life much meaning. I am now grateful for all the benefits I've gained from having been a worrier."

54.

When Two People Benefit from Each Other

*W*hen two people benefit from each other, how will this affect their being grateful?

If both have low levels of gratitude, each one is likely to claim that the other one gained more from him than he gained from the other. "He has a greater obligation of gratitude towards me than I have towards him," they will both claim.

Each one is more aware of his own time and effort spent to help the other. Each one focuses more on how the other one gained from him, rather than on how he gained from the other.

If, however, both people have integrated and internalized the value of gratitude, each one will focus on how much he gained from his fellow. Each one will focus on his own debt and feelings of gratitude towards the other. Each one will feel pleasure in expressing his own gratitude.

What will happen if two people benefited from each other but one feels gratitude while the other only expects and demands gratitude? The demander of gratitude will usually feel totally justified in his position. His colleague, however, might face a challenge. Some people in this situation might feel a bit resentful. "Just as I am grateful to him, he should be grateful to me. Since he lacks this gratitude, I won't be as grateful towards him as I otherwise would be."

A master of gratitude will still focus on his own obligation and responsibility to be grateful. "I certainly should be grateful. Whether or not this person is grateful to me is his issue with his character traits. That's his business, not mine."

A super master will focus on his own gratitude. He will be so grateful that he has gained from the other person that he will be happy that the other person has gained from him. It won't even enter his mind that the other person might not be as grateful as he should be.

Upon hearing this thought, some people might wonder whether others would take advantage of such a person, but he will not be if he is a wise, grateful person. He knows how to protect himself when necessary. Such a person's mind is full of thoughts of gratitude and appreciation. He will be a master of happiness, which is an integral part of his mastery of gratitude. He will live a joyful life. He will have the type of emotional life for which everyone else wishes. Practically, because he is so grateful to others, others will be happy to do things to help him whenever they can. If life were a game, he would be a true winner.

"I'm not going to be grateful to someone who isn't grateful towards me," someone complained bitterly to his rabbi.

The rabbi was working hard on trying to make peace between this person and a former friend. Each one was angry at the other for demanding gratitude without having a reciprocal feeling of gratitude. Both parties were strong willed and refused to budge.

One fellow seemed a bit more flexible than the other. The rabbi suggested to him, "Let's try something out as an experiment. Let's see what happens if you express your gratitude to him."

"How can I do that, Rabbi?" the fellow protested. "Then he will feel that he is right and I am wrong."

"First of all, doesn't he feel that way right now? So you won't be losing very much. In fact, he will probably have more respect for you for recognizing what he considers to be the truth. He might gloat a little, but, then again, there is a greater possibility that he might have a change of heart. You might be surprised to find that your gratitude towards him will cause him to be more open toward feeling grateful to you. On the other hand, if you both keep up your resentment towards each other, neither of you will have much to be grateful for in the future," said the rabbi.

The more flexible one agreed to give it a try.

"Thinking it over, I realize that I have a lot to be grateful for to you. I want to express my sincere appreciation for what you have done for me," the proactive expresser of gratitude said to the other.

He said this with authentic feelings of gratitude. To his amazement, the other man smiled and said, "I thank you for your gratitude. Now that I feel better, I realize that I have reason to be grateful to you, also. Please forgive me for being unreasonable before."

The next day, the one who had taken the initiative to express gratitude called the rabbi and told him, "You now have another example of the validity of your theory. I'm grateful to you for your persistence."

55.

Why Should I Be Grateful? He Enjoyed Doing It!

Some individuals tend to downplay a need to feel and express gratitude. They claim, "Why should I be grateful? He enjoyed doing it."

Every time someone does something for another person, he will have some reason for doing it.

For example, when someone visits another person who is in a hospital, if he appreciates the importance of visiting people who are ill, he will feel good about the visit. If he doesn't really enjoy going, he might be going because he is afraid that he will feel guilty if he doesn't go. Or he is afraid that he is likely to feel embarrassed if others will ask him why he didn't make the visit.

The person who enjoys going because he loves to do acts of kindness or because he is happy to do something for a person for whom he cares is on a higher level and deserves credit for it. Instead of decreasing our sense of gratitude, we should be grateful that this person has developed a love for kindness from which we have gained. If the person cares about us personally, this is a factor for which we can be grateful.

Our greatest obligation of gratitude for others is our obligation towards our parents. While parents enjoy doing things for their children, this doesn't lessen our obligation towards them. Rather, it increases it.

I once met someone who was a master at not being grateful to anyone for anything. "Anyone who ever does anything for me is doing it for his own agenda. So why should I ever be grateful?" was a comment he made frequently.

If anyone ever suggested that this person should be grateful to him for what had been done for him, the man would respond, "The very fact that you are asking for gratitude shows that your real motivation for doing what you did was because you wanted me to be grateful to you. That's exactly why I'm not grateful."

There are takers and there are givers in this world. This person was an extreme taker. Whenever he did anything for anyone else, his main motivation was for his personal benefit. Since he personally thought this way, he felt that others also thought this way. It was unfortunate that he lost out on the many spiritual, practical, and emotional benefits of someone who is an idealistic giver and has a heart full of gratitude.

56.

I'll Be Grateful After I Get All that I Want

Some people block their minds from focusing on gratitude because they say to themselves, "I can't be grateful yet. I want so many more things. I'll just have to wait until I have all that I want and then I'll begin to be grateful."

Their thoughts might not be phrased in precisely these words, but that expresses their basic attitude. This is an attitude that prevents gratitude.

This mindset makes it almost impossible for those who have adopted this outlook to master gratitude. They might feel grateful once in a while, but they will not master this attribute. There are always more things that one can want. There will always be things missing from one's wish list. Such a person will always be thinking, "I want more."

The reality is that we can be grateful even if only a fraction of our wants are reached. When we are grateful, we are happier and more joyful. The energy of these positive feelings gives us more inner empowerment. We feel more alive and energetic. When we feel this way, we are much more likely to make and reach more goals.

Our mindset comes from the thoughts we choose to think. When it comes to gratitude, we can choose one of two mental programs (with many variations in each one). One program can be called, "What I still don't have." The other program is, "What I can be grateful for."

We can run the gratitude-producing program even if there are a multitude of things that we don't yet have, and might never acquire. This way, we will become aware of what we can be grateful for.

Conversely, even if someone has a tremendous amount of things for which to be grateful, he has the potential to overlook it all by running the program, "What I still don't have."

If you don't consciously develop a positive program for yourself, you might be fortunate to spontaneously run a positive gratitude-creating program. But since our mental programs are started off in life by being programmed by an infant, then by a toddler, then by a young child, and then by a teenager, we need to be aware of what programs we are running now that we are older. And even if we are mentally running excellent programs, we always have the ability to keep upgrading our gratitude program.

The benefits of running a program that enables you to be grateful regardless of what you have is so valuable that it's worth all the effort it might take for you to master the mental mindset.

"I had heard about the importance of developing gratitude," a student told me, "but I didn't know how. I was often told, 'You aren't as grateful as you should be,' and those who said this to me were correct. I wasn't very grateful. Of course, if someone did something very special for me, I felt a bit grateful. But it was short-lived. Because of my lack of gratitude, I frequently felt bitter and upset that others didn't meet my expectations. My expectations were so high that I rarely was grateful.

"What can I do to improve?" the student asked.

He was told, "Our minds are truly amazing. We have the ability to train and condition our minds in the direction that we know is best. Going on automatic pilot, our minds might easily be selfish and self-centered. They can tend to focus on what we want, and not on gratitude towards what we already have. Tell your mind the following each day for at least a month: 'Mind, today keep your main focus on what you have and what you are grateful for. Throughout the day ask me the question, "What are you grateful for now?" If you don't think of an answer, then ask, "What could you be grateful for now if you were grateful for something?"'

"By gently getting your mind to focus on things for which you are grateful, you are creating the mental habit of gratitude. Be patient. When you keep this up, you will eventually find that your mind automatically focuses on gratitude."

The student followed through and became a much more grateful person. All who practice this will succeed at upgrading their level of gratitude.

57.

Humility and Arrogance

An arrogant person will lack gratitude. It takes humility to be open to acknowledging that we have gained and benefited from another person, so gratitude and humility go together.

An arrogant person is strongly biased. He wants to feel that he has done it all alone. Recognizing that we need others to help us accomplish takes humility. A humble person can be a truth-seeker. An arrogant person will try to bend reality the way he would like it to be.

An arrogant person will be afraid that if he expresses gratitude to others, others who hear about it will not hold him in the same high esteem that they would if they thought that he didn't need anyone else. A humble person doesn't consider it a high priority to have others view him as capable of doing everything on his own. And he certainly wouldn't want to gain any honor or prestige that he doesn't deserve. When he knows that others have helped him, he wants them to get the credit for what they have done.

A person with humility will be open to expressing gratitude to others who helped him, even when they only helped a little and he himself did most of what was done.

A person with humility doesn't feel a need to draw all the attention to himself. He will even appreciate the opportunity to share the limelight with others.

An arrogant person will want to give others the impression that he is the brightest, most talented, most clever, most creative, etc. If he thanks others for their input, he fears people might think that he isn't as intelligent and talented as they thought at first. This, however, doesn't concern a humble person.

Expressing gratitude can be distressful for an arrogant person, while a humble person experiences positive feelings that he is meeting his obligation by expressing gratitude. It's not that he needs to overcome the challenge of transcending negative feelings. The thoughts he thinks don't create any negative feelings towards giving thanks in the first place.

In short, upgrading your level of gratitude will also help you develop the wonderful attribute of humility.

Someone shared with me how ridiculous an arrogant person sounded when taking the credit for an accomplishment that was really a group effort. As he boasted in public about how amazing he was for all that he accomplished, he didn't seem to realize how much more esteemed he would have been in the eyes of his audience if he would have stated the truth: He could not have done it alone, and he is grateful for all those who contributed in many ways to make the accomplishment possible.

58.

Unrealistic Expectations

$\mathcal{U}$nrealistic expectations can be a reason why someone won't be grateful to another person.

Let's say that Reuven, who is in need of a large amount of money, is hoping that Shimon will give him fifty thousand dollars to assist him. For whatever reason, Shimon gives him only four thousand dollars. This would usually be considered a nice amount for which the recipient would feel grateful. If he wasn't expecting any money at all, the amount he did receive would make him feel good and he would feel and express sincere gratitude.

But Reuven expected fifty thousand dollars. The amount he received was less than a tenth of what he was expecting. He is intensely disappointed.

What will Reuven's thoughts be when it comes to being grateful to Shimon? It might be easy for him not to be grateful at all. Instead of gratitude, he might feel resentment.

Reuven needs to realize that his expectations weren't realistic. The proof that they weren't is that the only amount that was realistic in this case was the actual amount he received. The amount he was hoping for was just a wish. The stronger the assumption that he was likely to receive fifty thousand, the easier it will be to feel ungrateful for the amount he did receive.

A master of gratitude will be grateful whenever someone does something for him. He won't allow expectations and assumptions to prevent him from being grateful.

Even if you wanted more from someone — more time, more help, more money, more effort, more action, more words — be grateful for the time, help, money, effort, action, or words you did receive.

Someone who attended a school for a number of years lacked gratitude towards that school. When confronted about why he didn't feel more grateful, he replied, "I don't think that they gave me all that I needed. The teachers should have paid more personal attention to me. They should have spent more time to make certain that I was learning and growing as much as I could."

"Let's assume that you are one hundred percent right," a rabbi told him. "They should have given you more personal attention. They should have spent more time. But you still need to be grateful for what they did do for you and what you did gain.

"A person who feels that others didn't help him sufficiently, and therefore lacks gratitude, won't be grateful to G-d. There is a well-known statement of the Sages, 'Whoever has one hundred wants two hundred. Whoever has two hundred wants four hundred.' We all want more than we have. This means that the only way we can be grateful to our Creator is if we are grateful for the good in our lives, even though we wish for more.

"The same applies to the kindnesses of other people," the rabbi concluded.

The man agreed that this made sense. He then focused on all that he gained from the school. His appreciation grew with the passing of time and he eventually became a major benefactor of that school.

59.

The Problem of Procrastination Versus the Power of "I'll Do It Now!"

"*I*t's usually much easier to say to oneself, "I'll do it later," rather than, "I'll do it now!"

It doesn't take much effort to say, "I'll express my gratitude later." When "later" comes along, doing it even "later" means that it certainly won't get done now.

Nothing stops accomplishment like procrastination. Laziness and procrastination build on each other. The antidote is the trait that's called *zerizus* in Hebrew. This is the quality of doing things right away or as soon as possible.

When you think of saying something to someone to express gratitude, take action to say it as soon as possible. Say to yourself, "I'll do it now."

When you think of some action to take because you feel grateful to someone or to a group of people, do it right away. Say to yourself, "I'll do it now."

Every time you take immediate action, you will be building up your quality of *zerizus*. Thus, expressing gratitude as soon as you can builds up two qualities at the same time.

As soon as you finish reading this section, think of a specific thing you can do to express your gratitude to someone. Do it right away.

If you have a greater debt of gratitude to someone you can't speak to right away or can't write to at the present, as soon as you can, write down in a "to do" list what you will do and when you will do it. And find someone who is close by to express gratitude to right away.

"I'm a great planner," a middle-aged man told me with irony. "It's not that I'm skilled at making plans and following through. Rather, I'm an expert at saying, 'I plan to do this or that someday.' If only I would have carried out even ten percent of those so-called plans, I would have many significant achievements."

"What are some of the things that you did actually accomplish?" I asked him. After he answered, I asked what had motivated him to take action when he did follow through.

After thinking about this for a while, he said, "I had never analyzed it, but now I see that when I did take action it was always because I had someone as a mentor helping me along."

"It seems that your mentors had a very positive impact on you, didn't they?"

"They certainly did."

"I would suggest that you call up each of those mentors as soon as you can and tell them how grateful you are for what they have done for you. Do it today, and this will be a step in the right direction toward doing things immediately instead of procrastinating. Then, whenever you think of any of those mentors, your mind will associate them with your being grateful and with your taking action to accomplish."

60.

When Someone Does Something Imperfectly for You

*W*hen someone does something imperfectly for you, you will have to make a choice. One choice is to focus mainly on what wasn't done right, and could — even should — have been done better. The other choice is to focus mainly on what was done right, and to be sensitive about the wording of the correction.

When we have a gratitude consciousness, we will focus mainly on what the other person did that was helpful to us. We will have "a good eye." We will see what was done. We will see what was done right. We will see the other person's efforts. We will comment on how we sincerely appreciated what the other person did and did right.

Don't we have to point out what wasn't done right and what needs to be done better? Very often, yes. And we need to do it in such a way that our expressions of appreciation come first and stronger. Our gratitude needs to be clearly expressed and the recipient of our communication must clearly see and understand and feel that we are grateful for his efforts and thoughtfulness. We should sense his good intentions, and that will guide us in what we say. "Good intentions" have been maligned. In certain instances, the criticism of good intentions alone is appropriate. But in most instances, sincere good intentions should be recognized and positively commented on.

When the person who did something imperfectly hears and sees that you are grateful for the positive aspects of what he did, this will enable him to feel better about you. He will be more motivated to upgrade the quality of what he does.

Start off with words of gratitude. Let it be stated clearly that you are grateful. Then you can gently and sensitively point out what needs to be done better, either this time or in the future. When you point out the mistake or what wasn't done yet, don't use the word "but."

For example: "Thank you for what you did, but you did this thing wrong, and that thing wrong, and those things wrong." Rather, use the word "and." "Thank you so very much for what you did, and allow me to point out this detail that needs to be corrected."

What will be stronger in your mind, gratitude for the positive, or irritation for the negative? Regardless of what it used to be, now, in the present, appreciate your own opportunities to feel grateful and to express it. Allow your feelings of gratitude to increase and let them create the good will that they have the power to generate.

Someone shared his experience with me. His wife's wisdom transformed their marriage from a potential disaster into a harmonious relationship.

"All I remember from growing up was being criticized. My father and mother both were experts at finding fault with what I did. They were right. I did make many mistakes. I didn't always finish what I had to do. I was sloppy in the way I did things. But I had a defeatist attitude. I always assumed that no matter how hard I would try, I would do something wrong. And regardless of how much I would do and how well I would do it, the only thing I would hear was that I should have done it better. So this discouraged me from trying very hard. I felt it wasn't worthwhile. While I hated this pattern, I automatically modeled it. I, too, would invariably notice what someone did wrong and not what they did right. I might have paid lip-service to say, 'thank you,' but my heart wasn't in it. On the other hand, my criticisms were said loud and clear.

"When I first got married, I kept up my so-called family tradition. I would thank my wife for the positive things she did, and then elaborate on what she did wrong. To say that she hated this is an understatement. She grew up in a family that excelled in gratitude. When I joined their family, I could feel the good energy in the air. Mistakes were pointed out in such a way that the object of the 'criticism' barely felt it. And I noticed that the members of the family would correct what needed to be corrected efficiently and with good spirits.

"My wife was growing sadder by the day. When I asked her what was wrong, she would say, 'Nothing,' but it was clear that she was unhappy. Finally she said to me, 'You have so many good qualities that I appreciate, yet I am miserable. There's just one pattern that I would be extremely grateful if you could change. Your words of criticism and complaints are said often and strongly. Your words of appreciation are few and without life. I would be extremely grateful if it would be the opposite. I want to make you happy; please make it easier for me. Focus on what you appreciate and point it out. Then gently tell me what you would want me to do better. Let's discuss these points with mutual respect.' I appreciated the way she said this to me. I saw how much I appreciated the positive approach she used to point this out to me. I realized that this could have been said in a way that would cause a bitter argument. She said this so respectfully that I felt fully committed to communicating in ways that focused on how grateful I was.

"I followed through on my commitment. I, myself, was happier than I had ever been before in my life. My wife's wisdom and sensitivity gave us both a happy marriage and a happy life."

This was in stark contrast to someone who got divorced. The fellow acknowledged that it was his fault, but he only truly understood this after it was too late. He had claimed it was wrong to be grateful if someone did something wrong. He felt he had a holy obligation to constantly correct his wife. He was told by rabbis and counselors that he should be more grateful, but he just argued with them, "She should improve, and only then will I be grateful." He saw how miserable he felt being divorced and estranged from his children, who couldn't stand his constant barrage of criticism. "If only I would have been more grateful," he sadly said.

61.

Whining Prevents Gratitude

whiner will always find something to whine about, while a grateful person will always find something for which to be grateful. Whining prevents gratitude.

Since nothing we receive will ever be perfect, there will always be something to complain about. Since no person is ever perfect, a whiner will always be able to find fault with what someone has done for him. Everything done for someone could have been done better in some way. And even if a person is going out of his way right now to help you, far beyond the call of duty, you might be able to remember times and moments in the past when he didn't do all you were wishing or hoping he would do for you. So you can whine about his overall record, even though now he is doing something positive.

Whining doesn't start with your words. It starts with your thinking. Whining comes from the thoughts that you are not being treated as kindly and fairly as you would like. When there is a strong valid complaint, it would not be considered whining. Whining is when you take a minor thing that went wrong and build it up out of proportion. Whining is when you have a lot to be grateful for but instead of being grateful, you focus in a negative way on the trivial things that weren't to your liking.

Whining is when you yourself are to blame for what went wrong, and, instead of taking responsibility for it, you place the blame on someone else. Often that someone else is someone towards whom you truly owe a debt of gratitude.

We can all notice the negativity of whining. This is especially so when someone who should be grateful towards us whines about something we said and did, or didn't say and do.

Even when we are grateful to someone, we might still want to make constructive comments to improve a situation. When this is the case, communicate in ways that are mutually respectful. Focus on the outcome you want. Ask yourself, "What is my goal right now?" Then ask yourself, "What can I say to reach the outcome I want in a respectful manner?"

"Why do you complain all the time?" a young married fellow was challenged by his wife of six months.

"Me, complain?" he replied. "I don't complain all the time. As a matter of fact, I rarely complain."

"You're denying reality," she retorted. "I hear you 'kvetching' all the time."

The two of them decided to speak to an objective outsider to get a more realistic picture of their patterns.

The rabbi they consulted listened carefully to what they were both saying to get a comprehensive picture of the situation.

He pointed out to the wife that saying that her husband complains "all the time" was an exaggeration that prevented him from listening to the truth in what she said.

He pointed out to the husband that while he doesn't complain "all the time" he does have a strong tendency to complain about things. The husband defended his pattern by saying that everyone in his family spoke that way, and that it seemed the most natural thing in the world to him.

The rabbi suggested that both of them focus on what makes them feel grateful. The husband should verbally express his gratitude at least ten times a day for a week. And the wife should verbally express that she is grateful for her husband's expressing gratitude.

A week later, they reported that this was the best week of their marriage. They appreciated each other more than ever before, and were much happier than they usually were.

The husband said, "This positive approach helped me realize that I did tend to complain much more than I thought I did. And I noticed the great difference in my life when I made a conscious effort to express gratitude as much as I could."

62.

What Have You Done for Me Recently?

*T*here is a anti-gratitude attitude that can be summarized with the question, "What have you done for me recently?" This has become such a cliché that some people say this jokingly. But the general attitude that is contained in this sentence conveys a thought that prevents gratitude.

True, someone might have done something for you a while ago. But what has he done recently?

Someone might have given you a job or suggestions on ways to become financially successful a few years ago, but recently he has not been helping you out.

Someone might have gone out of his way to visit you when you were ill or in a hospital, but recently he hasn't done anything special for you.

Someone might have spent a lot of time and energy being there for you when you needed help, but recently he has been busy helping other people and hasn't given you the time you would like.

Your parents might have done everything for you when you were a child, but now that you are an adult, they feel that you should manage on your own. They don't do for you all that you would like them to do.

A master of gratitude focuses on thoughts and feelings of gratitude because of the good that was done for him. Time doesn't play a major role. Even if the good was done a long time ago and has not been repeated recently, a person who excels in the attribute of gratitude is still full of gratitude.

The attitude of a master of gratitude is, "If you have ever done positive things for me, I will remain grateful for the rest of my life."

I met someone who used to be very grateful towards certain people a number of years ago. But now one could easily see that he wasn't grateful any more. I was sitting near him at a bar mitzvah when someone asked him about it. "How come you aren't as grateful towards these people as you used to be?" that person asked him.

"I'm only grateful towards those who keep on helping me in the present," he replied. "When I first became religious, I needed their help. Lately, I haven't been around them very often. I'm more grateful towards the people who are helping me out now. My needs have changed since then."

The person who challenged that individual replied in an understanding way, "It makes sense to me that right now your feelings of gratitude are stronger for what is new and present-oriented. But that doesn't mean that you should forget your debt of gratitude towards those who helped you in the beginning of your spiritual journey. Just the opposite; now that you have a greater awareness of how they have benefited you, you can increase your feelings of gratitude. Feeling gratitude for those people won't diminish your gratitude for the people who are helpful to you now."

I could see from the way the recipient of this message reacted that he accepted the validity of it. He said, "You are right. I am grateful to you for pointing out to me that I should be more grateful to those people."

63.

"But I Don't Have Anything Special to Say"

Some people tend to push off writing notes of gratitude because they feel that they don't have anything special to write. Similarly, they might hesitate to make a telephone call to tell someone that they are grateful to him because they feel they don't have anything special to say.

Write or speak from the heart. It's more important to express the gratitude that you truly feel in simple, plain language than to push off writing or speaking because you can't think of a fancy enough way to convey it.

When you express your heartfelt feelings of gratitude, the authenticity of your message usually comes through. The recipient feels that you are truly grateful and is likely to appreciate it. One does not need to be a gifted writer or speaker to express gratitude. It is better to use a standard statement of, "Thank you very much," than to wait until you have moments of poetic inspiration that never seem to materialize.

With special people and for special occasions there are professionally printed cards with messages of gratitude. Even though you aren't the original author of the message, the fact that you went out of your way to buy the card and mail it shows that you are truly grateful.

Someone who realized that she had been lax in expressing gratitude went to a store that sold greeting cards and bought fifty cards. She had planned to send cards to only six or seven people, but she figured that even if she would only use three or four more of the cards it was worth the financial investment to have the ones that would be used. After mailing the first seven cards, each day for over a month she realized she was grateful to more people who she thought would appreciate receiving a card.

One elderly person wrote back a few weeks later, "I want to thank you so very much for sending me such a nice card. I hung it up in a place where I would see it often. It's such a great feeling to know that someone feels grateful to you. Do you do this frequently?"

The response of this person motivated her to do it much more frequently than she had before.

64.

Truly Loving Kindness Versus Loving the Gratitude of Others

The highest level of loving kindness is to do kindness for others without any focus on the practical benefits you personally will gain from the recipient's gratitude. When your motivation is to emulate your Creator and His kindness, you love the kindness you do even if gratitude is not expressed. When your motivation is to do kindness out of love for other people, you will be joyful that you have an opportunity to help someone, even if he won't be grateful.

Some people have the attitude, "If someone lacks gratitude for what I do for him, I'm not going to do things for him." Yes, when you do kindness for someone, that person should be grateful. But even if he isn't grateful, you still have done something great by being kind. And the more difficult it is to be kind, the greater the act. Knowing that someone won't be grateful makes the kindness more difficult. For this reason it is greater.

There are many instances when someone won't be able to be grateful. Attending someone's funeral is called *chesed shel emes*, a kindness that is true. The deceased will not be able to thank you for going out of your way to come to his funeral. He won't give you any gifts for your kindness. He won't help you out in any tangible way. And he won't reciprocate by coming to your funeral (may you live a long and healthy life).

How can we tell if our motivation for kindness is out of a love for kindness or out of wanting someone to be grateful to us? When we choose to help the one who needs our help the most even if he won't be grateful over the one who needs our help much less but will be grateful, then we see that we were motivated by wanting to do kindness.

What if we see that we are motivated by the wish that someone will be grateful to us? The Sages teach us that we should do good deeds even if our motivation isn't on the highest level. When we consistently do good deeds, it becomes part of who we are, and eventually we will upgrade our motivation.

"I went out of my way to help this person and he didn't tell me he was grateful," complained someone who did many acts of kindness for others. "It's important to me that when I do something for another person, he expresses gratitude. I don't know if I'm going to help him again."

"Are you serious?" I asked him.

"I certainly am," he responded. "I'll do anything I can for another person, but only if I know that he will be grateful."

"You appreciate the great value in being a kind person, don't you?" I asked him, knowing that he is tremendously kind. There were very many instances in his life where he did things for others that most people wouldn't do. He had a true love for kindness — but it was conditional.

"Very much," he replied.

"If someone hasn't yet developed the attribute of gratitude, why should you allow that to stop you from being a kind person? You gain so much from being kind that you shouldn't let someone else's limitation stop you from being all you can. The reward for kindness is eternal. Gratitude feels good, but it's nothing compared to the Almighty's eternal reward. It's nothing compared to the profound light that your soul gains from your kindness. Don't allow someone else's lack of awareness to rob you of those benefits."

"Put this way, I can see the validity of your argument. I thank you for pointing it out to me."

65.

Won't Gratitude Spoil People?

Some people are afraid that if they express gratitude to others for the good that those people do for them, those people will feel so good about the gratitude that they have already received that they won't keep doing good.

This is an interesting thought. There are only two problems with it. One, the opposite is true. When gratitude is expressed to people for the kindnesses they have done and services they have rendered, they are *more* likely to do more acts of kindness and to continue to render more and better service.

Secondly, we each have an obligation to express our gratitude to others and our focus needs to be on our obligation, rather than on an imaginary problem that this could cause.

In line with the argument that gratitude might spoil people, someone might say, "If this person gets used to others being grateful, won't this cause him to expect gratitude more often?

Then he will suffer disappointment when he doesn't get gratitude. So I will be doing a positive service by not expressing gratitude, to prevent him from getting used to it."

It's an interesting excuse, but it's not valid. You can't hold back the gratitude that this person deserves with the rationalization that your gratitude will cause him disappointment when others aren't grateful. That would be like a person saying that he shouldn't do acts of kindness for others. If he does acts of kindness, that person will expect those acts of kindness and will feel more disappointed when others don't do the kindnesses to which he became accustomed. When we love to do acts of kindness, we focus on what we can say and do to make another person's life better. The fact that someone else might not do the same won't serve as an excuse for not doing the kindnesses we can do.

It's more likely that when we express our gratitude to someone, our gratitude will serve as a role model for this person and he will increase his own gratitude to others. And when he expresses gratitude to more people, it is likely that others will express more gratitude to him. Instead of causing him more disappointment, we are likely to cause him to receive more gratitude in the long run.

I once spoke to someone who grew up without gratitude. He was expected to meet his obligations in the house and no one felt the need to be grateful to him for anything he did. He had a strong feeling that he wasn't appreciated, and this had a generalized negative effect on his entire emotional life. When he became a husband and father, his natural tendency was to refuse to express gratitude to his wife or children.

His wife felt that their children would lose out a lot if they didn't hear words of gratitude. She insisted that she and her husband both express more gratitude to their children. At first he argued that this wouldn't be good for the children. But his wife gently and patiently pointed out that children who grow up with gratitude were happier children and had a greater love for doing kindness.

The husband argued that if he were to express gratitude to his children for what they did, they would be motivated to do positive things out of gratitude and not because it was the right thing to do.

They ended up speaking to a Torah scholar who told them, "Expressing gratitude to your children will increase their own emotional health and give them a more joyful life. They will be more grateful themselves and this will give them greater gratitude to the Almighty."

The husband began expressing more gratitude. In a relatively short time, he acknowledged that he saw the benefits of expressing gratitude. At first, he did this out of respect for the rabbi they had spoken to, but then he realized that the limitations that he had grown up with had stunted his spiritual and emotional growth. He now realized that by his expressing gratitude to his children, he was benefiting them spiritually and emotionally.

66.

Express Gratitude Rather than Guilt

*S*ome people tend to express guilt when others do things for them. You will hear them saying things like, "I feel guilty for having bothered you"; "I am so sorry that I made you go out of your way"; "I feel bad for having taken your time"; "Please forgive me for your having to do this for me."

People with this pattern are often sensitive people who don't want to cause others any distress or unpleasantness. Sometimes, they could use a boost to their self-image. By realizing that they have infinite value and worth because they are created in the image of the Almighty, they will increase their realization that they deserve the kindness and goodness that others do for them.

When someone talks this way, he is unwittingly creating negative energy for himself and for the person he is speaking to. The words we say create the energy we experience. When someone says that he "feels guilty," "feels bad," or is "sorry," he is creating negative energy for himself. Similarly, the person he tells this to might feel bad or guilty that he is causing someone else bad or guilty feelings. (When someone actually caused another person a loss or pain, he is obligated to apologize and ask for forgiveness. The guilt is appropriate and the distress is a stepping-stone to elevating oneself.)

When someone goes out of his way to do something for you or helps you in any way, express gratitude rather than guilt. When you say, "I am so very grateful for all the effort you put into this," or "Thank you very much for having done so much for me," you experience the positive energy of feelings of gratitude. And the person you are telling this to will experience positive energy for being appreciated.

Many people who use expressions of guilt and of being sorry in these types of situations aren't aware of how frequently they speak in this pattern. Reading this will help them upgrade their pattern. Their awareness of needlessly expressing guilt will help them remember to genuinely express positive words of gratitude. Both the speaker and the listener will gain.

When someone told me that he feels guilty that he took my time, I pointed out, "I feel bad when you feel bad that I spent time doing something for you. If you don't want to, you don't really have to say that you are grateful. But please don't feel guilty. It was my free-will choice to do what I did for you. I am happy that I was able to do it. If you want to say something, I would appreciate it if you would say that you feel grateful."

The person smiled when I said this to him. "I didn't realize that I was causing myself negative feelings whenever someone did something for me. Now that I hear this, I can see why I always try to avoid asking other people for help even when I really do need their help."

A few weeks later this person reported to me, "Since I began expressing gratitude instead of guilt when people are kind to me in any way, my level of happiness has gone up. I see that I am feeling better and I am making other people feel better. I have pointed this pattern out to a couple of other people. I told them that I used to have this guilt pattern until recently and that it's so much better to express gratitude instead."

67.

Center of the Universe Complex

There is an attitude that is sometimes referred to as a "Center of the Universe Complex." This is when someone feels that everything centers around him. His mindset goes like this: "Of course, people do things for me. They should. Everyone should. And therefore I have no need to be grateful to anyone. Everyone who does things for me is doing exactly what they should be doing and I don't have to feel grateful."

On one level the basic idea that "the universe was created for me" is a correct concept. As the Talmud (*Sanhedrin* 37a) states, "A person is obligated to say, 'The world was created for me.'" But this is not meant to be a source of selfishness and self-centeredness. Just the opposite; this is a statement that we are responsible for the world. We need to think about what we can do to help the entire world. Of course, we are all limited in time, energy, and resources. But we should do as much as we can.

A self-centered person isn't grateful. He is more likely to have complaints that others aren't doing enough for him. As a matter of fact, there is never enough that others can do for him. If they would do things for him day and night, there would still be more that they could do. And a self-centered person won't be a truly happy person. He is a taker and not a giver.

Givers' attitudes can foster in them a sense of gratitude for what they receive. They are grateful for opportunities to do kindness for others. This will provide them with many opportunities for doing positive, meaningful things that give them joy.

Someone told me that he almost got divorced, but at the last minute his marriage was saved. He related, "As a child I didn't do anything for anyone. I was an only child and my parents couldn't do enough for me. They never let me do things and spoiled me rotten. I got anything I wanted. I had no tasks or duties to do in my house. My mother or father would do it all. I grew up with the attitude that everything was coming to me and there was no need to be grateful to anyone for what they did for me. When I met my future wife, she seemed like a very kind person. And I thought to myself, 'She will be like my mother. I won't have to do anything for her and she will do everything for me.'

"I was taken by surprise when after a year of marriage she told me she was totally miserable. She worked hard and I never uttered a word of gratitude. I didn't help out in the house no matter how tired she was. If I was lazy but appreciative, it would be bearable. But all she got were complaints that she didn't do enough, and what she did, she didn't do fast enough. She asked me to go for counseling but I refused. I viewed her complaints as immature. That is what she was there for: to serve me. She should be so happy that she was married that she shouldn't have any complaints.

"When the rabbis at the Rabbinical Court heard the entire story, they told me, 'Your wife does so much for you, how can you not be grateful?' 'That's her job and obligation,' I defended myself. But they told me that I needed to develop at least a minimal level of gratitude. If not, I wouldn't be able to make a future marriage work either.

"'See if you can become more grateful,' they said to me. 'Let's meet again in a month.' That night I couldn't sleep. I realized that they were right. My wife did do a tremendous amount of things for me. I should have been grateful. I apologized to her from the bottom of my heart, and told her that I resolved to be grateful. And I would do more things for her. She was skeptical and said, 'Seeing is believing. Words are cheap. Unless I see a change, the marriage is over.' That hurt. But it was understandable.

"By the end of the month, she saw in action how I was deeply grateful to her for the many things that she did for me. I helped her in ways that I wouldn't have believed I would ever do. What's more, I felt so much better about myself for improving my character.

"That was more than a year ago," he said. "And I have a happy marriage. My wife is happy with me and I am happy with her. I see how close I was to ruining my life. I am grateful that the wake-up call I received actually woke me up."

68.

Height of Ingratitude

"Height of ingratitude." This morning this was the pre-headline in smaller type above a larger headline in a daily newspaper. Since I am presently working on the topic of gratitude, it immediately caught my eye. What happened?

A 27-year-old new father was arrested for stealing the cell phone of a doctor. The doctor was in the process of saving the lives of his newborn premature twins. Their lives were in danger and the doctor was totally engrossed in doing all he could to ensure the physical safety of these babies. The physician was successful and their lives were saved. Instead of being grateful, the man broke into the doctor's room and stole his telephone. An alert guard in the hospital noticed something suspicious and the man was arrested.

Yes, this man was highly ungrateful. But there are many common examples of gross ingratitude. Aren't many children (of all ages) lacking gratitude towards their parents who have given them life and done so many things for them?

What about lifelong friends who have helped each other a great deal but are now involved in a quarrel? Where is their gratitude towards each other for the multitude of things the other one did?

What about a married couple who has done thousands of things for each other, but complain, argue, and even fight over relatively minor disagreements?

It is easy to notice the ingratitude of someone else. And especially if someone is ungrateful to us, we will feel strongly that this is wrong.

The ingratitude that is most important for us to be aware of is our own ingratitude. The question we should ask ourselves is, "In what ways am I ungrateful to someone towards whom I should be more grateful?"

And the ultimate ingratitude: Being ungrateful towards our Creator, who has given us life and everything we ever had and have now.

Let us learn from the ingratitude of others to become more grateful ourselves. From now on whenever you see ingratitude, immediately ask yourself, "In what ways am I ungrateful? And what can I say and do now to be more grateful?"

On a bus I overheard someone complaining, "No one is grateful these days!"

"You're right," said the person sitting next to him. "The young generation lacks gratitude. My children are so ungrateful to me.

My boss is ungrateful. My friends are ungrateful. Gratitude is rarer than pure gold."

I interrupted them, asking, "Could I please ask you both a question?"

"Certainly," they said.

"I would like to ask a question, but I am afraid that you might get angry at me for asking it."

"We won't get angry," they both said.

"Great! What are you both grateful for?"

They both thought for a while, and then gave answers. Then one of them said with a sheepish grin, "I see that it's a lot easier to complain about the ingratitude of others than to increase one's own gratitude. Thank you for pointing that out to me."

69.

Feelings of Gratitude Can Go Up and Down

Feelings of gratitude, like all other feelings, won't stay still. They tend to go up and down. They can get stronger and weaker. Moreover, even when thinking about the same individual, it's possible that sometimes you think about the good that he has done for you and you experience feelings of gratitude towards him, and a day later, or even an hour later, you think about something that this person didn't do for you, causing you to lack feelings of gratitude.

Gratitude consists of thoughts. But besides being a pattern of thought, gratitude also consists of feelings. Don't expect them to stay at the same level. If at any given moment you lack the feelings of gratitude that you once felt before, this doesn't mean that they have disappeared. They still exist in your brain's mental library. But experiencing them in the present can become stronger or weaker.

Repetition of the thoughts of gratitude can increase the strength of those feelings. The more you think about the specific things for which you are grateful, and how much you have gained and benefited, the stronger those thoughts become. Even if at a certain moment those thoughts don't add up to actual feelings, those thoughts can be available to you in the future. In future moments, your emotional experience of those thoughts can come back to you with added strength.

When your feelings of gratitude are strong, make a mental note of how you feel. Be aware of what you are telling yourself, what you are mentally visualizing, and the nature of the feelings that you feel. To come back to these feelings at a different time, mentally put yourself back into this same scene with all of its aspects. Hear what you heard and tell yourself what you told yourself, the same way that you did when you felt strong feelings of gratitude. Mentally picture the same things that you saw in the same way. And allow those same feelings of gratitude to flow the way they did when they were strong. Some people find this easier to do, and for some people it takes patience to gently allow themselves to adapt this way of thinking and feeling. Since this is an experience and not a concept, just reading about it is insufficient. It needs to be experienced yourself.

"I feel bad that I don't feel as grateful as I want to feel," a young man told his rabbi.

"Are you trying to feel grateful?" the rabbi asked him.

"I certainly am. I am thinking about gratitude and I wish that I would actually feel grateful," he replied.

"Your sincerity is clear and I see that you are doing what you can. Add words of prayer to Hashem. Ask Him to give you feelings of gratitude. Be aware of moments of breakthrough when you do feel grateful, even if only a little bit. Every moment of gratitude adds up. Most likely you will eventually experience more gratitude. But even if you don't end up feeling the way you want to feel, the very strong desire to feel grateful is elevating, and for this you have a right to feel better."

70.

Ask Other People What Makes Them Feel Grateful

A powerful question to ask other people is, "What makes you feel grateful?"

Most people are grateful for many things, but this isn't necessarily on the forefront of their minds. It's as if the thoughts of being grateful are on the hard disk of their mental computer, but not on the screen of their minds. By asking someone, "What makes you feel grateful?" you bring up the thought of gratitude on his mental screen.

After some people answer this question, you might add a statement like, "You are fortunate for that." "That's a wonderful thing to be grateful for." "So you always have something to be grateful for."

Be careful not to ask this question to someone who will become annoyed or irritated by your asking this question. Timing is important. At one time this question is exactly what this person needs to hear. At another time, it would not be appropriate to ask it.

When you build up the habit of asking people, "What makes you feel grateful?" you will find it easier and easier to do. Moreover, some of the people you regularly ask this question to will associate you with their being more grateful. That's a wonderful association to create. They will consistently feel better every time they see you.

You can ask, "What makes you feel grateful?" to people you know well, and you can even ask strangers who seem to be open. Many people begin conversations with others when they are both waiting in a slow-moving line. Have you ever seen someone turn to a total stranger and say, "The weather's really hot today, isn't it?" Or, "The line is moving slowly today. Why can't they make it go faster?" If people can kvetch to strangers, they can certainly express gratitude.

For instance, "Isn't it great that they have such a large selection of food to choose from? It's important not to forget to be grateful, isn't it?"

Or, "It takes a bit longer in the line here, but we can be grateful that they will take their time to answer our questions patiently when we need to know something, can't we?"

With some people, it might be best to add, "You don't have to tell me your answer. Just think of it in the privacy of your inner mind." Some people will be grateful to you for your sensitivity.

I am frequently asked, "What can I do if someone starts speaking negatively against other people and I want them to stop?

They won't listen to me if I just tell them not to say it." Others feel too shy or unassertive to simply say outright, "Please don't speak against another person. It's not right."

Often changing the topic of discussion is the best way to prevent negative speech from being said. One question that will help change the topic is to ask, "What makes you feel grateful?"

When you ask, "What makes you feel grateful?" some people will flexibly let go of the needlessly said negative speech and think about their gratitude. Others might be puzzled, "Why are you asking me that now?"

You might reply, "I love to ask this question. I learn from them what I can be more grateful for."

When the person you save from speaking negative speech gains a greater appreciation for how you are helping him spiritually, he will be more grateful towards you.

Imagine that you knew that someone would be grateful to you for how you were helping him. He would say to you, "I realize that you were trying to stop me from speaking negatively against another person. I am extremely grateful to you. Thank you so very, very much." Wouldn't that make it much easier to prevent negative speech by asking this question? Realize that this person's soul is grateful to you — eternally grateful.

⟨⟩⟨⟩

A student of mine with a tendency to be shy found it difficult to start up a conversation with people he didn't know well. He told me he would like to be more outgoing. "What would you suggest?" he asked.

I explained that the pattern of fear of being assertive and speaking up is based on pure imagination. By imagining that it will be difficult to speak up and that the other person will be critical, even angry, you create needless nervousness and anxiety. Realize that even though this feels difficult to you now, you will be able to melt the fear.

I told him, "Mentally picture yourself approaching people, speaking up, and enjoying the entire process. On the practical level, every day for a month look for opportunities to ask five people what makes them feel grateful."

"I could never do something like that. I'm not the type," was his initial reaction.

"If you find this too difficult, you can introduce the question by saying, 'I'm doing research on gratitude. Would you mind if I asked you to tell me a few things that make you feel grateful?' The worst that will happen is that the person might say, 'Yes. I do mind!' If so, apologize. Be grateful that he didn't yell and shout at you (if he didn't) and go on to ask someone else. You'll see that this just gets easier as you act on it."

He reported to me that many of the people he asked enjoyed answering the question and they even thanked him for asking them. He found his own gratitude awareness increased, and he now knows that it is really much easier to ask people questions than he had previously imagined.

71.

"Mirror, Mirror, Do I Look Grateful Now?"

The next time you feel the joy of authentic gratitude, look in a mirror. Remember this look. Even if you try to forget the imprint of that joyful gratitude, that look is stored in your brain forever.

Whenever you want to see that look of gratitude again, look in a mirror. Either you will see the look of gratitude again or you won't. If you do, great! If you don't, then adjust your facial muscles until you see the look of joyful gratitude once again.

You may ask, "But isn't gratitude based on my thoughts?" Yes, it is. The look on your face has a tremendous influence on your thoughts. Think great thoughts of gratitude and that influences your facial muscles; lo and behold, you look grateful. So, too, see the look of joyful gratitude on your face and you will find it easier to think grateful thoughts.

Question: If it's so easy to create the look of joyful gratitude on one's face by looking in a mirror, why doesn't everyone do this?

If you are really interested in finding out the answer, do a research project and ask people who don't do this why they don't.

But if you are already asking people about mirrors and gratitude, it's preferable to master this ability yourself. Then you can tell others, "I put the look of gratitude on my face when I look into a mirror. It works for me. It will probably work for you."

When I gave a seminar on mastery of one's emotional states, someone told me: "When it was suggested to me to see the look of gratitude on my face while looking in a mirror, I said to myself, 'This is ridiculous. It won't work. This is superficial. This is pop psychology. I'm much too sophisticated to increase my happiness this way. I'll feel foolish doing this. I wouldn't want anyone else to see me trying this out. I'm certain I won't let this work for me.'

"The person I argued with just said, 'Dr. Harvey Ekman is the world expert on facial expressions and emotions. His years of research have proven that this works for happiness and joy. It's your free-will choice. You can choose to prevent this from working for you or you can let it. You want to appear sophisticated. But to me it seems stupid not to utilize this scientifically proven approach that will help you live a more joyful life.'

"I didn't like the way I was spoken to. But I had to acknowledge that it made sense to test it out objectively. I knew that I could mentally prevent this from working and I could seemingly 'prove' it wouldn't work. But deep inside I knew he was right. I'm grateful for his taking such a strong approach. It worked wonders for me."

72.

Intensify Your Will to Become Grateful

$\mathcal{M}$ ake it a high priority to become a person who is consistently grateful. Let this be an important goal. "Nothing stands in the way of a strong will." This principle is the source of the success of successful people. Those who achieve excellence in any area need to have a strong will to take action.

If you are not yet a person who has mastered gratitude, intensify your will to do so. The stronger your will, the more likely your success.

Studies show that people who make goals are much more successful at whatever they do than those who don't make goals. Without making a formal study of it, it appears quite obvious that there are many more people who make it their goal to make more money than there are people whose goal is to master gratitude. However, a person who has great wealth will still be unhappy if he hasn't also mastered gratitude.

When a person hasn't become successful in a certain area, there are a number of possible reasons. One is that he lacks natural talents that would enable him to be successful. Another is that he doesn't have enough knowledge and information to know "how to." But a key reason in the vast majority of instances is that he does not consider that area a high-priority goal. People lack intensity of will when something that takes effort isn't deemed very important.

Increase your intensity to reach the goal of mastering gratitude. We all want to be happy and joyful. This is only possible with gratitude. When you know clearly what you want, and have a powerfully strong desire to get what you want, and what you want is not dependent on any other person, you will achieve what you want.

So if you are not yet grateful from the time you wake up in the morning until you go to sleep at night, it means either that special circumstances prevent you from experiencing gratitude, or that you are not as highly motivated to master gratitude as you could be.

Whenever you hear the word "goal," say to yourself, "My goal is to be a master of thinking grateful thoughts." The Almighty wants you to succeed. As long as you are determined to do so, you certainly will.

"I don't know why I'm not very grateful," a student said to me. "I want to be grateful, but I'm not. I don't understand why. If I want it, why don't I have it?"

"Did you ever meet someone who said that he wants to become more scholarly, but he isn't? Did you ever meet someone who want to have more money but he doesn't have as much as he says he wants?"

"Of course; many times."

"A general principle of life on this planet is, 'The way a person wants to go, he is led" (*Makkos* 10b). You need to strongly, very strongly, want something, to be led in that direction. If you just wish or hope that you will master gratitude, it isn't sufficient. Many other thoughts and actions will override those wishes or hopes. But when you have authentic, intense determination, you will succeed."

"But what can I do on the practical level?"

"Every day, twice a day, for five minutes at a time, look in a mirror and repeat over and over again, 'I am totally committed to mastering gratitude. I will think thoughts of gratitude from the time I wake up in the morning until I go to sleep at night.' Say this with tremendous enthusiasm and energy. Repetition and strong emotion together work wonders. Be willing to do this daily until you automatically find yourself being grateful throughout the day. If someone isn't ready to devote just ten minutes a day to this, he might want to become more grateful, but it's definitely not a high enough priority for him."

73.

Find a Gratitude Partner

*W*hen we work with a friend as a partner in self-development, we have added strength. A friend serves as a reminder. A friend encourages us when we need encouragement. A friend gives us positive feedback when we are on the right track. A friend makes the process much easier. This is true in all areas of our personal growth. And a friend can help us become a more grateful person.

Think of a person you feel comfortable with whom you can ask, "Would you be willing to serve as my gratitude partner?"

Ask your gratitude partner to remind you to be grateful for all the things for which you can be grateful.

One possibility is for your gratitude partner to ask you each day, "What are five things that make you feel grateful?"

Some people will be open to doing this once a day. But there is no law against asking each other, "What makes you feel grateful?" a few times a day. If you can't think of new things that make you feel grateful, you can be grateful for the same things over and over again. The reality is that those who do this will find more and more things making them feel grateful.

People who have gratitude partners are grateful to them for their help in becoming more grateful.

Being a gratitude partner for others will increase your own gratitude. As you regularly ask someone else, "What are five things that make you feel grateful?" you will find yourself remembering more things for which to be grateful.

There is no limit to how many gratitude partners you can have. The more you have, the more you will be doing a kindness for others, and you will add to your own gratitude.

Someone told me, "There was a person I cared for a lot. I felt that this person was creating a lot of unhappiness and misery for himself by frequently talking about what he didn't like. Whenever I met him, he would start off by telling me about many trivialities that were bothering him. His frequent talking about these irritating but inconsequential matters kept them at the forefront of his mind. I spoke to him a number of times about trying to become a more positive person, but I didn't make much progress. When I heard about having gratitude partners, I immediately said to myself, 'If I would be able to get him to become my gratitude partner, it would very likely have a positive influence on his becoming a happier person.'

"I wasn't sure that he would agree to become my gratitude partner, but I felt a strong drive to try. I first visualized myself asking him to become my gratitude partner. I mentally pictured him agreeing. I increased my own level of resolve and determination to have him become my gratitude partner. I said to myself, 'Regardless of how many "No's" he might give me, I will persist until he agrees.'

"At first he did refuse. He gave all kinds of excuses why this wasn't for him: It wasn't spontaneous. It wouldn't be helpful to him. It wouldn't last. He would feel silly doing this. He's not the type to do these kinds of things. It would just remind him of all the negative things in his life. He has many other attributes and qualities that he needs to work on. He never heard of anyone else doing this.

"When he ran out of all the reasons why this wasn't for him, I calmly and gently said, 'O.K., let's try it out and see what happens.' He repeated some of the excuses he had said before. And then I said, 'This will only take us a few moments at a time. I have decided that we will be gratitude partners. If you don't want to do it for your own benefit, please do it as a personal favor to me.'

"He reluctantly agreed. After a few weeks, he told me, 'I didn't think that this would help me at all. I am surprised by how much I gained. Thank you so much for not accepting my refusal. I feel that I have become a much happier person because of doing this with you.'"

74.

Before Falling Asleep

$\mathscr{S}$ome people find it easy to fall asleep. And some find it more difficult. Either way, everyone will gain from reflecting on thoughts of gratitude before falling asleep. End the day with the question, "What made me feel grateful today?" or, "What am I grateful for right now?" or, "What have I been grateful for at any time during my life?"

As you think about gratitude before you fall asleep, you will gain a greater level of awareness of the abundance in your life for which to be thankful. You will end the day with positive thoughts about the people to whom you feel grateful. And you will finish off with thoughts of gratitude to our loving Creator for His kindness.

When you reflect on gratitude before you fall asleep, there is a greater chance that you will have dreams that mirror this theme of gratitude. Some people will find that this happens quite soon. Others will need to keep this up for a much longer span of time. Be persistent and you, too, will dream dreams of gratitude.

Use your imagination to picture yourself dreaming grateful dreams. This way you are starting the process. Your dreams are dreamt in your inner mind and, as you store more gratitude imagery in your mind, those images will be brought to the forefront of your consciousness. And they will pop up by themselves in your daydreaming (if you daydream) and your sleeping dreams (which we all have, whether we remember them or not).

Realize that as you think of gratitude right before falling asleep, those thoughts will be repeated many times in your sleep since they are the last thoughts you think about at the end of the day. This is a powerful way to develop your quality of gratitude and integrate it into your consciousness.

A ten-year-old boy who had a difficult time falling asleep asked his mother what he could do about his problem.

"Is there anything bothering you?" asked his mother.

"Once in a while I have scary dreams and I feel afraid of them."

"As you lie down, say to yourself sentences that begin with, 'I am grateful for … .' Think of one thing at a time that you are grateful for. Think of the good things Hashem has brought you in your life. Think of anyone who has ever said something nice to you or done something kind. They might have done this recently or a long time ago. You might even repeat the same things each night or many times that same night. Allow yourself to feel happy for all the good that others have done for you."

After a number of nights of applying this exercise, the boy found it easier to fall asleep. This had a positive effect on his happiness level throughout the day.

75.

Gratitude Exercise (for Children)

This "gratitude exercise" will have a positive effect on those who practice it regularly.

The title states that it is "for children." It's for children of all ages. Those who feel that it's too childlike for them, because they are too serious to try something like this out, might be surprised by how much they will gain from applying it.

You might read this to a young child. Besides helping build the child's level of gratitude, you will be building your own gratitude.

[Touch forehead]

"I am grateful for my mind that thinks good thoughts."

[Touch near eyes]

"I am grateful for my eyes that see good things."

[Touch ears]

"I am grateful for my ears that hear good things."

[Touch near mouth]

"I am grateful for my mouth that speaks good things."
[Raise hands]
"I am grateful for my hands that do good things."
[Move feet slightly]
"I am grateful for my feet that walk to do good."
"I am grateful for all that can make me grateful."

76.

Associate Gratitude with Happiness, Joy, Bliss, Ecstasy, and Euphoria

*W*hen you say and think that you are grateful, how good do you feel? An obvious answer is: "It depends on what I am grateful for. The higher the value of what I am grateful for, the better I feel."

Whatever else we are grateful for at any given moment, at that moment we can be grateful that we are alive and we are breathing. So every moment of gratitude even for seemingly minor matters has an element of our being able to be grateful for the greatest things in our life. Moreover, the fact that we are alive means that we can be grateful at any given moment for everything that is positive in our life in any way.

Taking all that we have to be grateful for at every moment gives us a right to feel tremendously wonderful at every moment that is appropriate. The challenge is in accessing positive feelings of this magnitude. Isn't it natural that as we get used to things we don't feel as grateful as we did in the beginning? Yes, this is natural. And there is a way to increase our level of good feelings that we associate with gratitude.

Focus on this, because if you allow this tool to work for you, it will have a tremendously positive effect on your entire life. It is truly possible. The prerequisite, though, is patience and persistence, and you must be calm and open-minded about applying it in an effective way.

The effectiveness is based on the fact that the words we say affect our emotions. Even if we don't say words out loud, but only think them, they affect our emotions. This is seen clearly when a person is connected to an EMG, which measures the electric flow in the muscles. Each word we say either makes our muscles more relaxed or more tense, as can be measured with the proper equipment.

The following steps make this work:

1. When you feel grateful for anything, say or think, "I am grateful for this. I am happy that I am grateful."

2. Associate joyful feelings with the word "gratitude." How? When you feel good about something for which you are grateful, say the words, "Gratitude, Happiness, Joy, Bliss, Euphoria, Ecstasy." These are six words that your brain associates with good feelings.

3. To keep building up the power of these words, whenever you feel especially good feelings, even if these feelings are not at first associated with gratitude, say the words: "Gratitude, Happiness, Joy, Bliss, Euphoria, Ecstasy." Say them calmly and gently.

For example, if you are happy at a wedding where there is music that makes you feel good, feel grateful for the opportunity to be there and say, "Gratitude, Happiness, Joy, Bliss, Ecstasy, Euphoria."

Every time you repeat this when you feel wonderful feelings, you are strengthening the level and intensity of the feelings that you associate with "gratitude" and the five words that go with it. Words affect us because of the experiences we associate with those words. That is why those who speak different languages have different sounds that they associate with the feelings that go with those words.

Eventually you will be able to say this at any speed. It is advisable to begin your mental conditioning by saying the words very slowly — but realize that we are talking about only a few seconds longer.

What if you can't find anything to feel joyful about? What if you don't have joyful memories from your life history that you have associated with the positive feelings that are possible to associate with the six words?

Then use the power of your imagination to create joyful feelings. Imagine ten great things happening to you. Do this calmly and patiently. When you are able to create good feelings using your imagination, repeat slowly, "Gratitude, Happiness, Joy, Bliss, Ecstasy, Euphoria."

A note for those who feel they don't have this kind of imagination: Anyone who ever worries about anything that will happen before it has actually happened is using imagination to create an emotional reality. Some people have even been known to feel anxiety about some imaginary worry that never ultimately happens. If you can do this to create anxiety, you might as well practice using this to feel good instead of bad.

Imagine now that you have mastered being grateful. Imagine that your life is full of happiness and joy because you are consistently grateful. As soon as you are able to create positive feelings about this mental vision, say gently to yourself: "Gratitude, Happiness, Joy, Bliss, Euphoria, Ecstasy."

Let the story that goes here be your story. Apply this technique until you find it upgrading your entire emotional level. After it works, you will have a story about how this tool helped you. Be patient. It might take time until it works for you. Then you can share this tool with others who will enhance their lives by applying it.

77.

My Personal Gratitude List

*K*eep a list of the major things you are grateful for in order to read and reread it often. Since this is a list that you will keep adding to, you can place a few sheets of paper right here.

1.
2.
3.
4.
5.
6.
7.
8.
9.
10.
11.
12.